D0629573

Praise for *THE 85% SOLUTION*

"Now, more than ever, we all need to know that we can't blame the economy, weather, Wall Street, etc., for the situation we are in. We need to stop pointing the finger, look in the mirror, and muster up the courage to realize and admit it all starts with our thinking about personal accountability, which eventually turns into our reality and results. *The 85% Solution* masterfully demonstrates that a mind-set of personal accountability is where it all begins! The message is now ingrained in my brain and has changed my life!"
— **Irene Perez Zucker**, president, Verbacom Executive Development

"This book gives practical advice for your personal and professional development, pertinent in today's world. Galindo inspires you to choose your attitude and behavior and to live with those choices."
— **Stephanie Grenfell**, nurse manager

"In an engaging and humorous style, *The 85% Solution* provides the key to finding and defining success and living the life you've only dreamed of."
— **Janet Buchanan**, Buchanan Consulting

"You feel like you are there as you read Linda Galindo's examples, like someone filmed your life and showed it to you and suddenly it all became oh-so-clear why the misery and frustration in your life is of your own making."
— **Andrew Thweatt**, president, SKS, Inc.

"Change your life! Follow Linda's lead in moving from the Queen of Victims to a life of *accountability*. This book is written in a way that anyone can understand, enjoy, and most important, get the results you want, be happier, and lower your stress."

—**Jona Raasch**, president, the Governance Institute

The 85% Solution

HOW PERSONAL ACCOUNTABILITY GUARANTEES SUCCESS—NO NONSENSE, NO EXCUSES

Linda Galindo
with Versera Performance Consulting

Foreword by David A. Costello

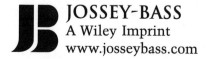

JOSSEY-BASS
A Wiley Imprint
www.josseybass.com

Published by Jossey-Bass
A Wiley Imprint
989 Market Street, San Francisco, CA 94103-1741—www.josseybass.com

Readers should be aware that Internet Web sites offered as citations and/or sources for further information may have changed or disappeared between the time this was written and when it is read.

Limit of Liability/Disclaimer of Warranty: While the publisher and author have used their best efforts in preparing this book, they make no representations or warranties with respect to the accuracy or completeness of the contents of this book and specifically disclaim any implied warranties of merchantability or fitness for a particular purpose. No warranty may be created or extended by sales representatives or written sales materials. The advice and strategies contained herein may not be suitable for your situation. You should consult with a professional where appropriate. Neither the publisher nor author shall be liable for any loss of profit or any other commercial damages, including but not limited to special, incidental, consequential, or other damages.

Jossey-Bass books and products are available through most bookstores. To contact Jossey-Bass directly call our Customer Care Department within the U.S. at 800-956-7739, outside the U.S. at 317-572-3986, or fax 317-572-4002.

Jossey-Bass also publishes its books in a variety of electronic formats. Some content that appears in print may not be available in electronic books.

Library of Congress Cataloging-in-Publication Data

Galindo, Linda A.
   The 85% solution : how personal accountability guarantees success : no nonsense, no excuses / Linda Galindo; with Versera Performance Consulting ; foreword by David A. Costello.
      p.   cm.
   Includes bibliographical references and index.
   ISBN 978-0-470-50016-3
   1. Business ethics.   2. Responsibility.   3. Leadership.   I. Title.   II. Title: Eighty-five percent solution.
   HF5387.G35 2009
   174'.4—dc22

                                                                                            2009025594

Printed in the United States of America
FIRST EDITION
HB Printing   10 9 8 7 6 5 4 3 2 1

To Mike, Lea, and Kayla
You inspire me every day to live accountably, learn enthusiastically,
and laugh when I need to.

Contents

PART II Self-Empowerment

PART III Personal Accountability

Foreword

I watch the news, read the papers, and follow the Websites. They're all full of distressing failures, disappointing behaviors, dire economic results, and doomsday commentary.

Are you yet growing weary of the widespread irresponsibility, abuse of power, and accountability vacuum so prevalent among us? I am! And if you are, I invite you to join me in an exciting journey of responsibility restoration, self-empowerment awareness, and accountability makeover leading to your success and joy in your work and play.

Linda Galindo's book, *The 85% Solution*, is our starting point . . . and what a great orientation to an exciting journey.

In a style that reminds me of Ben Franklin's *Poor Richard's Almanack*, Galindo suggests that success is at least 85 percent of *my* doing, *my* attitude, and *my* being whom I should be.

The 85% Solution's practical guidelines for true success include:

- Responsibility: "Responsibility is not something you do; it's a way of thinking and a way of being."
- Self-empowerment: "Take the actions and take the risks that you need to in order to ensure that you achieve the results you desire."
- Accountability: "Accountable people put a 'who' with every 'what.'"

A refreshing and enjoyable distinction made by Galindo is the three-part assessment of the accountability quotient: responsibility, self-empowerment, and personal accountability. When completed, the quotient indicates one's strengths and areas for improvement and is a personal road map for achieving 85 percent and beyond in our quest for an accountability lifestyle.

With all the books at your disposal about success and responsibility, why in the world would you want to read *The 85% Solution*?

One reason is the author, Linda Galindo, a nationally recognized author, educator, speaker, consultant, and expert in executive leadership development. She knows what she's talking about because she lives responsibly and accountably.

Another reason for reading the book is the very practical guidance you receive in real-world settings and the void-filling encouragement you find on every page.

The 85% Solution not only answers the question, "How much of your success depends on you?" but it also places you on the journey of joy in achieving success more fully.

July 2009   David A. Costello, CPA
President and CEO, National Association
of State Boards of Accountancy
President, NASBA Center for the Public Trust

The 85% Solution

Introduction

You're lying on your stomach on a cold, metal gurney in an operating room, woozy from the anesthesia that will, in just a few moments, render you unable to speak or feel or react.

Four others are in the room, too: the orthopedic surgeon who will repair the errant disk in your back; the anesthesiologist who is monitoring your reaction to the medicine she just gave you; a circulating nurse who will watch out for your safety; and a scrub nurse who will pass sterile instruments to the doctor.

Through your haze you hear the two nurses arguing. One is chiding the other because she thinks the scalpels and clamps on the sterile tray have not been sufficiently cleaned.

"Mind your own business," the scrub nurse retorts. "I know how to do my job."

The circulating nurse takes her worries to the anesthesiologist.

"Leave me out of it," the anesthesiologist tells her. "That's not my responsibility."

So the nurse turns to the surgeon, but before she can speak, he snaps to the bickering group, "Quiet! It's time to start!"

As you lose consciousness, the scrub nurse hands a scalpel to the doctor, *who uses it to cut your back.*

Which of those four professionals is responsible for the safety of that scalpel?

Is it the scrub nurse whose job it is to sterilize it? The circulating nurse in charge of looking out for your safety? The anesthesiologist who rendered you unable to be responsible for it yourself? Or the surgeon who used it to slice through your skin?

Suppose you wake up from the surgery with a painful infection from the cut. Now who do you think is responsible? Which member of the surgical team will you hold accountable?

The scrub nurse? He believed the instruments were clean.

The anesthesiologist? She isn't in charge of the instruments.

The circulating nurse? She tried to tell everyone.

The surgeon? He didn't know anything was amiss.

If just one of these people is responsible, does that mean the others aren't?

Perhaps each of the four is one-quarter responsible for your infection.

Sound good? Next time you need surgery, will it be good enough to know that each person participating in a procedure that involves cutting your skin, touching your organs, or removing a diseased body part is willing to take one-quarter of the responsibility for making sure you don't die on the table?

I didn't think so.

Here's the only acceptable answer: Each conscious person in that room is 100 percent responsible for the success of the surgery, right down to the squeaky-clean sterility of the instruments.

If the scrub nurse was 100 percent responsible, he would have recleaned the instruments just in case the circulating nurse was right.

If the circulating nurse was 100 percent responsible, she would have prevented the doctor from cutting you with a dirty instrument by interrupting the surgery, even though the doctor told her to be quiet.

If the anesthesiologist was 100 percent responsible, she would have insisted that the scrub nurse resterilize the instruments as soon as she learned there might be a problem.

If the surgeon was 100 percent responsible, he would have invited the circulating nurse and the other team members to air their concerns before assuming it was okay to start the surgery.

Next time you need surgery, how responsible do you want each person on your surgical team to be for your well-being?

One hundred percent—each. No question about it.

Now apply that to yourself. Next time you agree to do something, how much responsibility will you take for it?

Here's the only acceptable answer: 100 percent.

When you work as part of a team at your job, be 100 percent personally responsible for the outcome of the effort—good or bad.

If you and your spouse have divided the household chores, be 100 percent responsible for how well your household runs, not just for your part.

In every relationship with family, friends, and coworkers, be 100 percent responsible for the harmony and health of that relationship, not just for half of it.

Even when you're working on something whose outcome matters only to you, be 100 percent responsible for it. Don't leave your success up to anyone or anything else.

Own it.

Not somewhat. Not partially. Not pretty much. Not, "I guess so" or "as long as." Own it 100 percent. No wiggle room.

I can safely guess that this is not how you operate today. Most people don't.

Most people believe they're responsible only for "their part" of a job, and that if someone else screws up and the project fails, it's not their fault. So why be responsible?

Let me tell you why: Whether you admit it or not, you *are* accountable for everything you're involved with, whether it turns out good or bad, whether it fails because of something you did or because of something your partners did. The outcome belongs to everyone who touched the project, not just to the ones who made mistakes.

You share or take all of the credit when all goes well. And like it or not, you are implicated in the blame when it doesn't, even if you're not the one who messed up.

It's just how it is.

Once you realize up front that the result is going to be yours no matter who does what to cause that result, you'll get better results—because you'll make better choices. And you'll be in control of your own success.

This shift in mind-set isn't easy, but it's worth the trouble. It will help you

- Get things done more effectively and with less stress
- Feel a sense of accomplishment in your job
- Develop stronger, more positive relationships
- Improve personal productivity and satisfaction
- Change your organization or your family for the better

You already have this ability, and you already have the responsibility; everybody does. But most of us either don't realize—or aren't willing to admit—that we alone have the power to live our lives how we want to.

No other person or unforeseen circumstance can do that for us or to us.

We can give other people and outside conditions power over us, but that's a conscious choice. It doesn't happen without our permission.

This message—this book—is important right now because we are bombarded every day with messages from guilty officials, celebrities, and even the media, who tell us that outside conditions have the *most* to do with what happens to them—and to us.

Keep reading. I'm going to convince you that *you*—and nobody or anything else—are accountable for what happens to you.

If you believe the environment, the universe, politicians, or other people are responsible for your success, *good luck*.

If you believe you're responsible for your own success, your luck is bound to improve.

Change your *mind-set*. Be responsible.

The truly good news is that each of us has 100 percent personal responsibility available to us as a mind-set.

If it is to be, it's up to me.

It's total personal responsibility. It's mine. I own it. There are no trap doors.

The critical factor missing from most of our lives is a mind-set of commitment and ownership to a result before we set out to do something, whether it's to get through our day, finish a home improvement project, or do our jobs.

What is your mind-set?

Your response to the following question will reveal the truth about you:

> How much of your success is up to you, and how much of it is determined by outside conditions, like the environment, other people, or just plain bad luck?

What's your answer? Forty percent you, 60 percent environment? Half and half? One hundred percent you, forget the outside world?

What your answer reveals is how successful a person you are.

If you answered 85 percent (or higher) you, 15 percent (or less) outside conditions, that says you believe that you are responsible for your own success. And I'll bet you're successful.

On the other hand, if your answer is 50-50 or anywhere less than 85-15, be honest: Are you as successful as you would like to be?

Or does it seem that other people, situations, and influences seem to always stand in the way of your getting ahead?

Deep down, do you know that they're not the ones to blame when you don't finish a project, achieve a good result, or come through when people are counting on you?

Deep down, do you know *you alone* are responsible for everything you choose to do?

Would you like to solve—or prevent—your problems? Would you like to be more successful? Would you enjoy feeling happier, more confident, and less burdened by worry and regret?

Here is your solution: Acknowledge, believe, and act on the fact that you, and you alone, are 100 percent responsible for your own successes, opportunities, and happiness. Just you and your choices, you and your mind-set. Not anybody or anything else.

Likewise, you, and you alone, are 100 percent responsible for your own failures, problems, and bad mood. You and your choices.

Too big a leap? Start at 85 percent.

Can you acknowledge that you are responsible for at least 85 percent of everything that happens to you, and that other people and conditions beyond your control are responsible for no more than 15 percent?

That's a mind-set that will help you improve your life so vastly that you will strive to be 100 percent responsible.

That is the 85% Solution.

Right now, you might think you know someone who could benefit from what I'm telling you: your spouse, a colleague, your best friend.

Go look in the mirror. That someone is you.

Stop blaming your problems and failures—big or small— on the people around you. Stop using "circumstances beyond my control" as the scapegoat for your own choices, behaviors and actions.

The 85% Solution will show you how.

In *The 85% Solution*, I guide you through a three-step process that will help you own your choices—all of them.

The 85% Solution will give you the tools you need to fully own your actions. It will offer you a tremendous opportunity to change the outcome of your work, your relationships, your career, and even your life by taking charge of yourself and then accepting the consequences for doing that.

To get there, you will have to take these three important steps:

1. Be responsible for the success or failure of everything you do—for your choices, behaviors, and actions—*before* you know how it will all turn out. Own all of it, even if you're working for or with somebody else.
2. Empower yourself to succeed. Take the actions—and take the risks—that you need to in order to ensure that you achieve the results you desire.
3. Be accountable for your actions. Demonstrate your willingness to answer for the outcomes that result from your choices, behaviors, and actions, without fault, blame, or guilt.

Responsibility, self-empowerment, accountability. These are the keys to taking control of your own success.

I ought to know.

PART I

Responsibility

The Queen of Victims: A Fairy Tale

Once upon a time, I was the Queen of Victims, with a shiny scepter, a sparkling crown, and a plush velvet robe, walking up and down the runway of Poor Me. Life didn't work for me. My boss was a jerk. My parents didn't encourage me. My husband was controlling. I got divorced. I complained and whined.

One day, a good and smart friend put a stunningly quick stop to it by asking me a revealing question that stung me like a slap in the face.

"Have you ever noticed that all the bad things you complain about happened when you were in the room? Have you ever considered that you might have something to do with your own rotten luck?"

I hadn't.

This so-called friend must have lost her mind. "What kind of friend are you, anyway?" I pouted.

Honestly, it never occurred to me that I might be inviting sadness, heartache, confusion, and struggles with the way I was behaving: irresponsibly. Every time I hit a rough patch, I had someone to blame: my boss, my parents, my ex-husband, my fair-weather friends, my hairdresser, my dog.

My good and smart friend's point was this: Bad things were happening to me because of my own actions, my own behavior, and my own pitiful Poor Me thinking, but I was crying so hard I couldn't see it through my tears. I had so many excuses about why my life was a mess, and so many people to blame.

After all, I *did* have an unhappy childhood; that couldn't be my fault. My boss *was* always yelling at me for something I supposedly did wrong—a clear sign that *he* needed a personality transplant. There's nothing I could do about *him*.

So at first, I thought my friend was nuts, or worse—I thought she was mean. Maybe she was jealous of me or had it in for me for some reason—with my luck, it wouldn't surprise me.

So I tried to prove to myself that what she said wasn't true.

I couldn't possibly be perpetuating my own failures. It was my boss's fault, my parents', my ex-husband's, not mine.

I clung to my status as Victim. *Queen* of Victims. *Proud* Queen. Right, not wrong. Always right, but never happy. Poor me.

Eventually, though, I could no longer deny that my friend was right, not jealous (why would she be jealous of someone whose life was a train wreck waiting to happen?), even though it hurt my feelings to hear her question and stung my pride to admit it was true.

When the wisdom of her comment finally sunk in, my life slowly started to change. I realized that more of what "happened" to me was due to my own choices than I was claiming or even willing to admit. Much more.

All of it.

I realized that I needed to *own* those choices, *own* my actions, and *own* the results of those choices and actions.

I needed to stop being a victim, turn in my crown and scepter, and understand that bad things don't just happen on their own; rather, they're the result of poor choices and thoughtless actions.

I had to realize that consequences flow from my own choices, actions, and behaviors. I needed to take control of myself, to be the leader of my own life.

I needed to realize that I wasn't my parents' or boss's or ex-husband's victim. I was my own. I needed to stop victimizing myself.

In short, I needed to be responsible for my life by being responsible for my choices and my actions—and the consequences that flowed from them.

I'll admit it was a little embarrassing to confess to my friend and even to myself—and eventually to everyone—that I had been sabotaging my own success and happiness, all the while blaming it on others so nobody (including me) would know what I was doing.

I was like those promising young marathoners who suffer one injury after another from overtraining and never win their races—but they have a built-in excuse for their failure: "It's not my fault."

I never accepted responsibility for my failures because I always had someone or something else to blame, and my excuses sounded legitimate (at least to me). I could say it wasn't my fault, and that excused me from being responsible for those failures. Or so I thought.

That smart friend of mine is a truly good friend. She told me what I needed to hear: that I'm in charge of this life of mine.

That means standing up and being responsible for my failures as well as for my successes—and, in fact, doing that *before* I know whether my choices and actions will result in success or failure.

It's easy to claim responsibility when things go well, but it's hard when they don't. A truly responsible person is responsible either way.

The most amazing part is this: The more I am responsible for my actions and choices, the fewer failures I suffer, and the more successes I enjoy. The more I am responsible for my own actions and choices, the better I enjoy the life I lead, going full-throttle or cruising or stopping short—whatever I decide.

I don't go a day without saying out loud: "I own this."

I'm responsible for my choices, my actions, and their consequences. It makes every day so much smoother, so much more directed, so much more likely to end without massive stress or upset.

Now I'm going to pass my friend's good deed along to you. I'm going to tell you what you need to hear: that it's time for you to be responsible and accountable for everything you do, even if it turns out that you did the wrong thing.

What are you blaming on others: rotten luck, lousy job, money problems, spoiled kids, failed marriage?

Were you in the room when any of those problems started?

Admit it: You are responsible for everything in your life. The choices you have made have resulted in these outcomes.

Own it: Every choice, every behavior, every action you take is yours. They're nobody else's fault.

Do it: Commit to accountability. Watch it rock your world.

It's My Responsibility

We stood in front of a black sign with white letters that read, "Please Wait to Be Seated," and we waited.

I was hungry and impatient, and not in any mood to wait.

Two couples who arrived ahead of my weary four-woman group waited, too, even though at least half of the tables in the restaurant were empty.

I took that as a sign that the restaurant's staff was slow and incompetent. That made me more impatient.

When we were seated and our food arrived, I lost it.

"You call this a fresh fruit salad?" I chided Lindsay, the nineteen-year-old waitress who delivered a bowl of faded honeydew and overripe cantaloupe that the kitchen had, for some reason, thought I would eat.

I expected Lindsay to tell me it wasn't her fault because she didn't make the salad. But she stunned me.

"No," she agreed, "it doesn't look fresh at all. The kitchen is just about out of fresh fruit. I'm sorry."

It's not often that I'm speechless, but at that moment, I didn't know what to say. I knew it wasn't her fault. Yet she apologized.

As my mouth hung open, Lindsay directed my attention to the plump, red strawberries that garnished the sandwich platters my friends had ordered.

"How about a big bowl of those?" she offered. I closed my mouth as it started to water.

She returned in a hurry, eager to salvage my supper. But steps away from our table, she stumbled over a kink in the carpet and released the bowl, sending strawberries flying all over my dinner companions and me. They landed in our hair, on our shoulders, on our laps, and even in our purses.

Speechless. Again.

"Did everybody get some?" Lindsay asked, and she started to giggle.

It infected all four of us. We howled.

This teenage ray of sunshine helped us pick berries out of our hair and sped back to the kitchen to slice up some more. This time, I got to eat them instead of wear them.

We left her a huge tip, this young woman who spilled food all over us.

As we left, I pulled her aside. "You didn't get upset because I didn't like my salad or even when you tripped. You didn't blame the kitchen or the carpet or us for arriving so late. You just handled it. How do you do that?"

Her response was mature beyond her nineteen years.

"I'm responsible for making sure you come back," Lindsay explained. "You'll base your decision on my actions."

She was responsible for every mess she made. She was responsible for serving me the wilted cantaloupe. She was responsible for tossing strawberries all over my friends and me.

I asked Lindsay one more question before I turned to leave: "Why were so many people waiting to be seated when we arrived, even though so many tables were empty?"

She replied, "They wanted to sit in my section, so they had to wait for tables to open up. You were just lucky to get one of my tables."

I hope I'm as lucky next time I eat there.

This clumsy young woman told me she learned this by watching her manager, whose section is always as crowded as Lindsay's is now. That profound example taught her that taking total responsibility for herself, her job, her relationships, and her behavior is the key to avoiding unpleasant outcomes.

Are you ready to learn that? Are you ready to *live* it?

You Are Responsible: A Before-the-Fact Mind-set

Responsibility. It's a blessed thing when all goes well, but a curse when nothing's going right.

The client *loves* the new sales campaign? It was *my* idea! He *hates* it? I *told* Jenkins that idea wouldn't work! The patient made a miraculous recovery? *I'm* her doctor! She's taken a turn for the worse? *That stupid nurse gave her the wrong dose of medicine!*

You can say you're responsible only when good times roll, but you won't fool anyone except yourself—and you might fall short even there.

On some level, you already know this. Why aren't you practicing it?

You are responsible for the results of your choices and actions whether those results are good or bad.

You are responsible for meeting your deadlines, even if unforeseen obstacles or conflicting priorities arise.

You are responsible for your own effectiveness, your own reputation, and your own satisfaction.

Yet when you fall short, you often blame it on other people and unforeseen circumstances.

That's not responsible.

Responsibility is the before-the-fact mind-set of ownership and commitment to a result. It's the power of your thinking before you take action.

Responsibility is the first prong of an important three-step process that's involved in every successful project, relationship, or life. Responsibility is the topic of Part I of this book.

Be responsible for the success or failure of the endeavor, for your choices, behaviors, and actions—*before* you know how it all turns out. Own all of it, even if you're working for or with somebody else.

Responsibility is not something you do; it's a way of thinking and a way of being. There are no rules that govern the correct way to be responsible for your actions; rather, it's a frame of mind.

You *are* responsible. You *decide* to accept that responsibility. You *believe* that the success or failure of the project is *up to you,* even if you're working with lots of other people.

Likewise, you *acknowledge* that there are some factors beyond your control.

Bad weather, for instance, could prevent a construction crew from finishing a house on schedule—so the responsible builder builds time for that obstacle into the schedule and acts promptly if it becomes necessary to renegotiate the deadlines. A flu-stricken coworker might leave your team short-handed just as you face an important deadline, so you figure out how to overcome the setback and deliver the work on time, because you are 100 percent responsible for the outcome.

Even truly responsible people sometimes miss a deadline despite their best efforts. When they do, they are responsible for missing the deadline.

They admit that they could have figured out a Plan B in case somebody got sick.

They don't blame it on a poor feverish friend and let him take the heat when he's feeling low. That's not going to get the project finished.

Instead, they figure out how to finish the job as quickly as they can with a stretched-too-thin staff, and they renegotiate the deadline. Then they get back to work. And next time, they're prepared to pitch in for someone who gets sick.

Why waste time blaming the flu?

Planet What Is

Nicole is a bright twenty-year-old who lives on Planet What Should Be.

She wants to be a writer, and she's got a knack for it. Since elementary school, she and her parents have had plans for her to major in journalism at a big university.

She has barely moved into her dorm room before her self-employed father learns he has cancer and won't be able to work for a year, and he has decided to stop paying Nicole's tuition.

She tells him she shouldn't have to drop out of school or pay her own tuition. He advises her to get a job and save enough money to go to school part-time.

So she gets a job in a shoe store. Too bad her supervisor has it in for her, and he fires Nicole after just two months because Nicole, prone to the sniffles, calls in sick nearly every Friday.

So Nicole gets out the phone book and starts cold-calling editors to ask for a job. Impressed with her resourcefulness, guts, and telephone manner, one of them hires her.

The editor tells Nicole she has promise and pays for her to take some classes to learn more about the job she's been hired to do. He gives her some entry-level work to do, but no major writing projects, which go to senior-level employees with more education and experience.

He lends Nicole a book to read about writing so she can learn the correct style and format, but Nicole doesn't think she needs to read it—she's a good enough writer already.

Nicole cries at work and says she shouldn't have to do entry-level work. She should have gone to college; it's not her fault she didn't. She doesn't give her all to the work she's been hired to do.

After three months, the editor fires Nicole for coming to work late and for skipping shifts, even though Nicole wasn't feeling well on those days.

In Nicole's mind, none of this should have happened.

Yet it did.

Nicole isn't basing her choices and actions on *what is*. She is reacting to what *should* be. And that's preventing her from getting what she wants.

People who live on Planet What Should Be rarely get what they want because they spend most of their time figuring out who's to blame for the mess they're in.

Where do you live?

When's the last time you said you shouldn't have to do something or that someone shouldn't react to your behavior the way that he did?

When's the last time you were able to change the past by saying it shouldn't have happened?

Isn't it time you moved to Plant What Is?

On Planet What Is, it doesn't matter what should have happened or what shouldn't have. It matters what *is*. You only have to react to what *is*.

That makes your choice a cinch. How do you want to react to the situation that *is?*

Living on Planet What Is saves you the trouble of figuring out who's to blame for what should or shouldn't have happened. There's no need to spend your time worrying about how things could have, would have, should have been *if only* something had gone differently. It didn't.

All you've got is what *is*.

Deal with what *is*.

Nicole is unemployed, unhappy, and unsuccessful.

She's leaving her success up to others, to the environment, to chance, to fate. That strategy isn't working out for her.

Is it working for you?

Put the 85% Solution to Work for You

Suppose a husband and wife work at exactly the same job. As they walk out of the house together in the morning, Husband believes that 60 percent of the success of the day's work belongs to him, and 40 percent depends on outside conditions: the boss's mood; how often the telephone rings; whether he gets a flat tire on the way to work; how well he slept the night before.

Wife, on the other hand, is consciously committed to having a successful day. She believes that 85 percent of her success depends on her, and just 15 percent could be motivated by outside sources.

It should come as no surprise when, over dinner that evening, Wife has a happier day to recount than does Husband.

Here's why:

She chose to ignore the boss's bad mood, or she simply accepted his crankiness and found a way to engage him in the task at hand.

She chose not to answer the telephone for two hours so she could work without interruptions and finish her project more quickly.

Because she slept poorly the night before, she chose to compensate by taking a brisk walk at lunchtime instead of sitting in the too-warm cafeteria, becoming overrelaxed and eating the comfort foods that she knows can make her sleepy.

She noticed that one of her car's tires looked low on air that morning, so she chose to swing by the service station—and sure enough, the mechanic found a slow leak and changed the tire.

She chose to take charge of her situation, her day, her progress, and her success.

She chose before she left the house in the morning to be responsible—at least 85 percent of the way—for the success of her own day.

In short, she chose to have a successful day, and so she had one.

That kind of attitude is available to everyone.

It's available to you, right now.

If you believe that you are at least 85 percent responsible for your success—and that just 15 percent of the success of a project or a day could depend on the way the wind blows—you'll get the results you're looking for.

The mind-set to be responsible can be measured on a scale that ranges from zero to 100 percent.

The higher percentage of ownership you believe you have when you begin your day, a project, or your job, the more success you'll have.

You determine your level of achievement in advance.

You've done this plenty of times before without even realizing it.

Say you're planning to go on vacation, but you've got piles of work to do before you go. You can adopt one of two mind-sets:

1. *I'll never get all of this work done.* It would take me three days to finish all of this, and that's if by some miracle I had no interruptions—nobody dumping more work on me and no telephones to answer. I'm supposed to leave for my vacation tomorrow morning. Either I'm going to have to leave two days late—and my husband will be mad—or I'm going to have to tell my boss I wasn't able to get my work done—and my boss will be mad.

Either way, I'm going to have this cloud hanging over me while I'm supposed to be enjoying my week off.

2. If I work efficiently, enlist the help of my assistant, tell everyone up front that I won't be accepting any new work before I leave and turn my phone off for a few hours and let voice mail take messages, *I can plow through this by the end of the day.* It's going to be intense, but it will be worth it to leave for my vacation on schedule with no unfinished business hanging over my head. My husband and boss will both be happy, and so will I.

In the first scenario, you're a victim—of yourself. (Want to borrow my scepter and velvet robe? I'm not using them anymore!)

You've decided that outside conditions—the overwhelming amount of work, the interruptions by colleagues, the telephone calls, the potentially angry spouse and boss—will determine how successful you are today.

Note that I say *you've decided*, because that's what you have done. You have determined in advance that you will fail to finish the work and leave for your vacation as scheduled.

You have chosen not to be responsible for the outcome of the day. You have decided that you are not 100 percent responsible for your success—not even close.

You don't own this day.

And just look how it turns out.

In the second scenario, you do own your day. Your vacation is important to you, and so are your husband, your boss, and your commitment to finish the work.

In this scenario, you decide up front that you can have everything you want. You claim ownership for making it all happen because you want it so badly.

You choose up front to work as hard as you have to in order to get what you want—and, like the 98-pound weakling who lifts a two-ton car to rescue the child it has rolled on, you're able to pull off an amazing feat—something that might have defeated you *if you had decided* up front that you couldn't achieve it.

You choose to create a strategy for overcoming outside conditions that might get in the way of your success.

Remember Chesley Sullenberger III, the level-headed pilot who safely glided Flight 1549 into the Hudson River in January 2009 and saved the lives of his 155 passengers? He didn't throw up his hands and say, "It's out of my control," when a swarm of Canada geese apparently collided with the plane's engines.

Instead, he was 100 percent responsible for landing the plane safely and saving his passengers. He came up with a strategy for overcoming outside conditions that could have doomed them all.

Like the hero pilot, you are 100 percent responsible for the outcome, for the success of your day.

I'm guessing that most of your days don't involve death-defying decisions.

More likely, you've used *The 85% Solution*'s tools when you wanted to buy a new car but knew it would be a struggle to save the money, or when you coveted a better job but feared you would lose the chance to someone with more experience.

You made those goals yours—and yours alone.

When you took ownership of the outcome—when you were 100 percent responsible for succeeding—you found that you succeeded. You knew nobody but you would be responsible if you failed, so you didn't fail.

Even if you were to fall short of your goal, you would know it was nobody's doing but your own, so it wouldn't feel so bad.

If, instead, you blamed—in advance of submitting the job application or going for the interview—your parents for not being able to afford to send you to a better college, or your last boss for not promoting you to a position that would have prepared you for the new job, you wouldn't have the can-do attitude—the responsibility *mind-set*—that you needed to get what you wanted.

You would be a victim (your own), and it would cast a pallor as dark as your bad mood over the job interview. Who wants to hire a victim?

Ninety-year-old Ian Thiermann isn't anybody's victim. After the retired businessman lost every penny of his $738,000 retirement fund to scam artist Bernie Madoff, Thiermann accepted a $10-an-hour job as a greeter at a California grocery store.

With or without his fortune, Thiermann is responsible for paying his bills. Blaming Madoff wasn't going to pay his bills.

Let me ask you again: *How much of your success is up to you, and how much of it is determined by outside conditions?*

Are you even close to 85 percent? Do you want to be?

Get Off of Planet Guilt

So all you have to do is be responsible for everything you do, and then you'll be happy, successful, and worry-free?

If only!

Obviously, making a major life change like this is not easy. You have to choose to do it. You have to decide if you want to do it.

It wouldn't surprise me if you don't want to.

Here's why: To be responsible—to get to a 100-zero or even an 85-15 mind-set, you'll have to shake some behaviors and words that might not be so simple to let go.

Our society doesn't talk in a formal way about what responsibility means or is. We don't deliberately learn it in school or even—unfortunately—on the job.

We certainly haven't learned it from political and corporate leaders or from sports heroes who tell the world they aren't responsible for their own missteps, that they did nothing wrong. Instead they say, "Don't blame us."

Even though these role models are in "positions" of responsibility, they deny they are the ones responsible for the outcomes of their own choices, actions, and behaviors.

They blame the trouble on others—an auditing firm, a boss, their staffs, their friends, a confusing profit-and-loss statement.

If the big story about those leaders involved an unprecedented success instead of a crash-and-burn failure, do you think they would still point to the auditing firm, the higher-ups, or the record-keeping and say, "Give *them* all the credit! I'm not responsible!"

I don't think so.

Yet we all understand what responsibility means when something goes *right*.

This is how most people define responsibility: *If it works, I'm responsible. If it doesn't, I'm not.*

You *love* the birthday gift I gave you? I *knew* you would! You *hate* it? *My assistant forgot to remind me to buy something until it was too late. It's her fault.*

People who live at peace with themselves and are fulfilled, at ease, and successful have a different definition of responsibility.

They believe: *If it works I'm responsible, and if it doesn't work, I'm responsible.*

In a society that punishes us for failing, that's a hard thing to do.

Being responsible, we fear, will come back and bite us on the behind. Yet punishment, fault, blame, and guilt really have nothing to do with responsibility.

They're as far apart as separate planets.

If you want to live on Planet Guilt, be guilty—that's fine with me.

Planet Guilt is the Land of Finger-Pointing and Blaming Others. If that's where you live, you have plenty of company, in the form of unintelligent life.

Even if you choose to live on Planet Guilt, *you'll* still know who's responsible for your choices and actions—*you.*

Living on Planet Guilt doesn't let you off the hook for your choices, actions, and behaviors. Feeling guilty, sorry, or even sick in the pit of your stomach doesn't in any way, shape, or form absolve you from being responsible for your choices and actions.

You can feel as guilty as a burglar caught with his gloved hand picking the lock of the bank vault, and you'll still be the only one who is responsible for your choices and actions.

Indeed, you can be totally personally responsible and still be at fault when something goes wrong. There's nothing wrong with that!

You have to be 100 percent responsible in order to continually improve yourself, your business, your family, your relationships, or your projects—even if that means you are to blame, admit you're wrong, and accept that it's your fault that the idea didn't work or the project missed the mark.

Admitting those things moves the project, the relationship, or the organization along so you can achieve your goals for it.

Admitting those things allows you and those you're working with to unload the baggage and avoid arguing for hours on end about whose fault it is that something didn't turn out as expected.

Admitting those things is *hard*. It can be embarrassing. It can mean you have to change the way you've always done things.

It's so hard that one CEO told me he would *never* admit it if he did something that wasn't in the best interests of his organization. His accountability, he explained, is to his contract and the law, not to his employees or shareholders.

The payoff of such an admission, though, is *huge.*

So be clear about what you're admitting, about what you are responsible for. Admitting isn't just mouthing the words. It is owning what you have said and done.

Accepting that you are responsible moves you along so you can achieve your goals and live happily and peacefully with yourself.

Still, we point fingers in an effort to deflect the blame from ourselves, even when we know we're at fault.

We don't want to lose any of our pay or the respect of our boss, the board of directors, our spouse, our friends, or our neighbors.

Don't even pretend that you don't do this; everybody has.

When was the last time you pointed the finger at someone else when you knew, deep down, that you were the responsible party?

More to the point: When was the last time you *didn't* do that?

Let's look at what happened to Leslie, who skated through college without cracking the books because she's so smart.

Her college grades were so good, in fact, that she got admitted into law school.

Talk about moving to Planet What Is.

In law school, you can't skate by on your wit and intelligence, even if those are qualities of a good lawyer. You have to study, memorize, and write in a specific, new way. You have to devote all day, every day to learning.

Leslie didn't do that. She chose to work part-time as a waitress to earn spending money. She chose to volunteer as a campaign manager for a friend who ran for office. She chose to nurture her friendships by spending every Saturday night socializing.

Within a year, she flunked out of law school.

She argues it wasn't her fault. The reason she failed, she says, is because she's not a good writer, and the school shouldn't hold that against her. She says her grade point average is almost as high as the minimum allowed, and the school shouldn't be so strict. She claims she would have been reinstated if the school hadn't sent her dismissal notice to her old address by mistake because she would have had more time to prepare her appeal.

What she doesn't admit is that she got what she deserved. That's too hard, too embarrassing, to admit.

As long as she lives on Planet Guilt and points fingers and deflects blame, she will feel unsuccessful, even if she gets accepted into another law school.

She'll never be successful until she is responsible for her choices.

If she bore deep enough, she might find that she chose to spend her study time doing things that she likes better than studying.

If she owns her choice to earn spending money, manage her friend's campaign, and nurture friendships, she might find that law school isn't really what she wants.

Maybe she is successful after all.

Her mind-set of guilt, fault, and blame is just preventing her from realizing it.

In fact, she is unclear about what she expects from herself.

What is your mind-set preventing you from realizing about yourself? Bore deeper. You're in for a surprise.

No Fault, No Guilt, No Blame

We would rather blame a problem on someone else—
even someone innocent—than admit that we made a
mistake.

And why not? People get rewarded for placing blame.

*No, officer, I wasn't speeding. She slammed on her brakes for
no reason and made me run into the back of her car. It wasn't my
fault!*

If the officer were to say, "That's okay, just be more careful
next time," do you think you would start driving more slowly?

I don't. You would have gotten away with speeding and
causing an accident, and your behavior wouldn't change.

Likewise, at work, we're paid to produce a result. If we fail
to come through and the boss says, "Just try harder next time,"
and pays us even though we do not produce the result, why
should we try harder?

If my child calls me "mean" when I carry out the consequences that I've promised for the behavior she has displayed—and I back off because I don't want her to think I'm mean—she learns that she can whine, complain, threaten to withhold love, and call me mean, and I'll reward that behavior by backing down.

If Nicole's boss at the shoe store had patted her on the back and said, "There, there, don't worry about coming to work when your nose is running," the pitiful girl would have continued to call in sick every time her hypochondria flared up.

People repeat behavior that is rewarded.

If John and Joan work together on a project that fails after they agreed to rely on an unproven technology, their boss probably is going to chew someone's head off. If John knows he can blame the failure on Joan and save himself a good chewing out, why not do it? The boss will side with John— reward him—so John serves up that irresponsible behavior, again and again.

One reason not to do it, of course, is that it is irresponsible and dishonest to lay blame on someone else for a failure in which you have participated.

But a better answer is that *it doesn't matter whose fault the failure is.* What matters is that everyone gets back to work and figures out how to turn that failure into a success.

Still, John wants it to matter, and so does Joan. Both want to save their own skin by blaming it on the other. They want someone to pay, just not themselves.

Isn't that what we're used to, after all? Isn't that what makes headlines? Whose fault is it, and how will the guilty pay?

The truth is *it doesn't really matter* if it's Joan's fault or John's fault. All that really matters is that the team can rectify the problem.

So what if Joan convinced John that they should use unproven technology? Is John less to blame for the failure because it wasn't his idea, even though he agreed to try it?

For that matter, is the boss any less to blame? After all, he assigned an important project to two people with a propensity to try something unproven.

How much time should the three of them spend pointing fingers, yelling, and hurting each other's feelings? How much damage should they do to their relationships before getting back to the task, figuring out what went wrong and how to fix it?

Think of it like this: If someone offered each of them (or you) $500 to stop pointing fingers and direct your energy to solving the problem and finishing the job, would it *still* matter whose fault it was?

I didn't think so.

If each of the three people involved was 100 percent personally responsible for the success of the project, they would spend no time at all pointing fingers, yelling, or damaging their relationships after the project's failure.

Each one would own the failure. Then they would get back to work.

In a perfect world.

Our world is more perfect than you might think. The natural order of things is to try, see how it turns out, learn from our mistakes, figure out how to do better, try again, and succeed.

Finger-pointing and blaming is unnatural because *figuring out whose fault it is won't get the work done.*

Let's live in a perfect world. Let's live on *Planet What Is.*

Being responsible doesn't mean things go well every time. Rather, it means we're committed to continually improving.

Being responsible means there's no fault, no blame, and no guilt.

It's a mind-set shift that says: Here's an opportunity to produce a good result. Let's get to work. If we succeed, we can all be proud. If we fail, we can learn and keep moving forward as a team. Let's get the work done. Let's learn from our mistakes until we succeed.

Blame keeps us all running in place, never moving forward.

It takes a lot of energy to figure out who's to blame, to point fingers, to convince everyone it wasn't your fault, and to make sure someone else takes the fall. That's wasted energy.

Instead, if something goes wrong at work or at home, with your friends or even while you're alone working on something that's important only to you, own it!

You have the potential to be 100 percent responsible, to blame nothing on outside conditions, other people, or unforeseen circumstances.

Use your energy to figure out how you can have the results you want, be happy, and enjoy low stress, not how you can deflect the blame from yourself.

Will you get beat up sometimes because you're willing to be responsible when something goes wrong?

Absolutely. People will say you were wrong and they were right.

I say, *So what?*

Is it more important to be right or to be successful?

Is it better to be right or to be happy, at peace, free from stress?

Is it better to be right or to finish the job? Or salvage a friendship? Or keep the peace at home?

Can you write, "I am always right," on your résumé? Where do you think that will get you?

Here's an idea: Let *everyone* be right.

If I'm working with you and we hit a snag in our progress, and you tell me it's all my fault, I'll say to you, "Yes, you're right. It's my fault. Now, let's fix the problem."

I don't care if it's my fault or if it's your fault.

Responsibility means there's no fault, no blame, no guilt.

I don't want to waste my time arguing; that won't get the work done or achieve the result we committed to.

I don't want to waste my energy figuring out which one of us is to blame; that certainly won't move us along.

I don't want to waste my time living on Planet Guilt.

Chances are, I have decided in advance that I am 100 percent responsible for the success of this project, and that means I choose to complete it successfully, whether I'm right *or* wrong.

I'm not going to do it all myself. I'm going to hold myself accountable for our success, and I'm going to hold you accountable for our success.

Because I have that mind-set, it's never more important to me to be right than to be successful.

It's rarely more important for me to be right than it is for me to be finished with the job so I can go home and enjoy my two delightful daughters.

And usually, it's not more important for me to be right than it is for someone else to be right, so I gladly abdicate.

You can be right. Now, let's get back to work.

"I Am Not Lazy, I Just Pretend I Am"

Maybe you're 35 years old, or 45 or 55, and it feels impossible to change your mind-set this late in the game.

Maybe being responsible for your actions—and the eventual consequences of those actions—sounds like it will create more work for you.

It might.

My client, Lynn, a finance executive for a hospital, feared that being responsible for her actions would be a burden, but she reconsidered after I told her that becoming 100 percent personally responsible had made my own life easier.

She was wearing that heavy victim crown, too, so she really had nothing to lose.

Here's what she wrote to me:

> Last night I realized something: I am not overwhelmed, but I have this pretense called being overwhelmed.

I run this pretense because it allows me to play small, which, in my mind, allows me to look good. By pretending to be overwhelmed, I can show others how "important" I am.

However, by pretending to be overwhelmed, I keep myself distanced from what is really important: making a difference. By pretending to be overwhelmed, I avoid responsibility.

At first, I thought I was just plain lazy. Now, I realize that calling myself lazy is just another pretense. I am not lazy when it comes to things that really interest me.

I pretend to be lazy because it allows me to avoid responsibility and accountability. Being responsible and accountable requires playing full out, and that frightens me because I may fail and that would not look good.

I need to get a life. To do that, I have to let myself be vulnerable, and that is where courage in the face of fear comes in.

This morning I was at the gym doing chest presses with my usual 15-pound dumbbells and I thought to myself, "What am I really here to do?"

My goal—at least what I told myself—is to be physically fit, healthy, and attractive. But I don't play full out at the gym. I lift 15-pound weights because I can lift them easily. I don't try anything harder.

Likewise, at work, I don't push the envelope. I do what's easy and doesn't cause much pain.

I was going to write a memo to my boss explaining that I cannot possibly get everything done that I'm supposed to do this week. I've decided not to write it. Instead, I am going to play full out here at work.

Today is my two-year anniversary at this job, and I know I have not been playing full out since I have been here. I am committed to playing full out from this point on.

Thanks for helping me think this through.

You know the really cool part of this breakthrough? I don't have to fight it anymore. It feels great!

Like Lynn, you can break through your "pretense"—the pretense of blaming it on others, of failing because you really never try to succeed, of fighting the day instead of owning it.

Or you can continue to live the lie of "How Do I?"

Lynn was asking herself, "How do I possibly get all of this work done?"

By the time she thought it through, she knew she was asking the wrong question.

A better question is, "Why don't I do what I know how to do?"

She knew how to get the work done: play full out. What she didn't know was why she wasn't playing full out.

It took some painful introspection and some hard, cold admissions, but now she knows why, and she has chosen to change her behavior.

How many times a day do you ask yourself or someone else, "How do I . . . ?"

"How do I tell my employee she is not meeting my expectations?"

"How do I enforce a tight deadline without making everyone mad at me?"

"How do I tell my boss I would be a lot more productive if he weren't such a grump?"

"How do I admit I took out a mortgage I could not afford to pay?"

"How do I get my kids to clean up their mess without sounding like a nag?"

When you ask someone, "How do I," do you think that person knows better than you how you should handle yourself? Do you really want someone else "shoulding" all over you?

Or are you making sure you have someone to blame in case the conversation or confrontation you're dreading doesn't go well?

Ask yourself a different question: "Why don't I just do what I know how to do?"

You know how to tell your employee she is not meeting your expectations. You also know it's not going to be any fun, and she might cry or get angry.

She might even say it's your fault—that you haven't been clear about what you expected.

Would she be right? Is that why you're pretending you don't know how to talk to her?

Asking yourself "Why don't I?" instead of "How do I?" allows you to enter the conversation better prepared.

You might practice what you're going to say: "I noticed that the report wasn't on my desk Monday morning when I expected it. Then I realized we had not agreed that Monday was a firm deadline. I'd like to make a clear agreement now about when that report will be finished."

You're responsible for your oversight. And you're making it perfectly clear what you expect from your employee—without blaming her.

Likewise, "Why don't I want to enforce the deadline?" is a better question than "How do I enforce it?"

Is it important for you to be one of the "gang"—and enforcing the deadline will reinforce to your "friends" that you're the manager and they're the subordinates?

Is it more important for you to be liked than to own your role as manager, even though you accepted the title and the big raise that goes with it?

Ouch! That's hard to admit.

Now you have another question to ask yourself: "If I do what I know how to do, what can happen?"

If you choose to have the conversation, enforce the deadline, confront the employee, what's the potential consequence?

You might get the report on time next time.

You might decide you don't want to be a manager anymore.

Both are more responsible than pretending you just don't know how.

Yes, people will get mad at you for asking them to be responsible and accountable, to meet clear expectations and honor deadlines. Yes, you may suffer a few embarrassing moments and have to make some tough admissions—with no reward.

In the end, though, you will own your day, your choices, and your success. You will be in control of your own success.

You already know how.

A Good Reason Not to Share

Every time I work on a project, I am responsible for it.

I am responsible for it if I'm working solo, and I am responsible for it if I'm working on a team.

I believe it's up to me to make sure the project is completed successfully, on time and with good results.

So if I'm 100 percent responsible for the success of the project you and I are working on together, does that mean you are not responsible for it?

The answer to that question depends on how much responsibility you are willing to accept for the success of the project before you start it.

Remember the medical team in the Introduction? How much responsibility did each one accept before starting surgery with a dirty scalpel?

How much responsibility you accept at the outset of any project depends on how responsible a person you are.

It depends on how important it is to you that a project to which you are assigned is completed successfully.

Most important, it depends on how important it is for you to be successful, happy, fulfilled, and at peace because you know you're responsible for your own choices and actions.

Every member of a team is 100 percent responsible for the success of a single project.

The team is responsible for the project, but so is each team member. That is, team members are collectively and individually responsible at the same time.

Here's an example. Sarah, John, Bob, and Grace, all middle-level managers in the accounts payable department of a major health care organization, have been assigned to create a system for making sure the group isn't paying bills it doesn't owe, overpaying those it does, or making duplicate payments to vendors.

Sarah, who is new to the organization, helped create a similar system for her last employer; she emerges as the group's leader because she is outspoken and enthusiastic about her ideas for creating the new routine.

She adopts the mind-set that she is responsible for the success of the project, and she welcomes the opportunity to take charge.

She asks the team members if they are willing to work with her to implement a monthly audit of invoices—a system that would require someone in the accounts payable department to cross-reference every invoice with its purchase order and follow up with the people who received the merchandise to make sure they got what they paid for.

The system, Sarah assures her team, has the potential to save the health care organization several million dollars a year.

This is John's first professional job, and he has no experience with audits, but the idea sounds like a winner to him.

Grace is a long-time employee, but she has never worked anywhere else, and Sarah's idea sounds like it will put a stop to overpayments and duplicate payments.

John and Grace happily agree to Sarah's plan and leave the meeting feeling absolved of further responsibility. Sarah, after all, has experience and know-how, and she seems willing and capable enough to get this thing done.

Bob, on the other hand, has reservations about Sarah's proposal. He has worked at several other places, and he knows how time consuming it can be to do regular internal audits.

He fears the accounts payable department is understaffed for the task, and he knows the boss isn't going to hire a new employee to take on the extra work.

He thinks a regular audit is a great idea but would prefer to outsource the responsibility to a third-party auditor—a firm that would match up the payments, collect overpayments and duplicate payments from the companies to whom they were made, and deduct a portion of the refunds as its fee.

That way, the health care organization would still reap millions of dollars in refunds, but it wouldn't have to stretch its own staff so thin. The outside audit firms work on commission, so technically, it wouldn't cost the organization anything to use one.

Still, Bob keeps his objections to himself. After all, everyone else seems to like Sarah's plan, and Bob doesn't want to be the one to send the team back to square one.

That would make him unpopular and create more work for everyone.

Besides, the team might want him to take charge of finding the outside auditor or to become the team leader, and that might shift more work to him.

So he secretly objects to Sarah's plan but doesn't voice his concerns or offer his alternative plan. He leaves the meeting without praising or rejecting her strategy.

The next day, Sarah asks Bob to create a list of vendors to whom the organization makes monthly payments. He tells her he has another project to finish, so he won't be able to help her.

She turns to Grace, who tells Sarah how to create the list herself.

Finally, Sarah asks John, who says he'll try to fit it in by the end of the week, but it might be quicker for her to collect the information on her own.

So Sarah collects the data, writes the proposal, and schedules a meeting to present the plan to the boss.

John, Grace, and Bob attend the meeting. Sarah outlines her plan to create an internal audit system and save the organization millions of dollars.

John and Grace beam as she makes her enthusiastic proposal, counting on sharing the limelight even though they didn't pitch in with the work.

Bob keeps quiet . . . until the boss cuts Sarah off mid-sentence to ask, "Who on our staff has time to do all of that extra work?"

Sarah responds that her team—John, Grace, and Bob—will split the work.

That's when John stands up to say, "I won't be able to take on the extra work because I already have a full schedule."

Grace pipes up with, "I can't do it, either. We'll need to hire a new person."

The boss says there's no money in the budget to hire a new employee. He tells the team to go back to the drawing board and admonishes the foursome to cover all the angles next time. He tells them to have a new plan by the end of the day, even though Grace was scheduled to leave early that day to start packing for her vacation.

As they leave the boss's office, Bob says to the team, "I could have told you that we couldn't pull this off in-house." *It's not my fault.*

Grace, who was in favor of the idea, grouses, "This isn't fair. It wasn't my idea to try to put all of the extra work on us!" *Sarah is to blame, not me.*

John adds, "Sarah, that idea of yours wasn't such a good one after all." *You're the guilty party.*

Sarah is hurt, confused, and angry—and none of her emotions is about the failure of the project.

She is hurt that her teammates are blaming her for the failure—even though they all seemed to agree with her strategy when she proposed it.

She is confused about why, if they knew the staff couldn't handle the added work, they didn't offer their alternative suggestions during the start-up meeting and give more guidance.

She is angry that they refused to help her, pushed their part of the work off on her, and told the boss they would not do the additional work that would be required of them if the department began internal audits.

She's too angry to listen to Bob when he says the solution might be to hire an outside auditor.

The meeting erupts into a finger-pointing session. No more work gets done.

What went wrong?

Sarah decided at the outset to take full responsibility for the success of the project, and when her teammates fell short, she picked up their slack. So why didn't it work out as she hoped?

The team made two fatal errors.

First, Sarah, the enthusiastic leader, didn't realize that teamwork requires the work of each member of the team, and that one team member can't do the work of any of the others.

Second, John, Grace, and Bob did not take any responsibility for the outcome of the project, leaving everything up to Sarah and then blaming her for the inevitable failure.

If Sarah is responsible, we don't have to be.

Wrong!

All for One, One for All

In order for a team to be successful, each member of the team must be equally responsible—100 percent—for its success. One person can't be responsible for another.

Too often, responsibility is a zero-sum game. If I'm responsible, you're not.

That never works.

Here's what *does* work: I am totally responsible, and so are you.

Like the players on a basketball team, each member of any team plays an equally important role.

The star shooter can take shots only if the point guard passes the ball to him. He will be able to get close enough to the basket only if the center sets the pick that holds the other team's big guy at bay.

If the star is having an off day and isn't hitting his shots, the team can still win the game if each player plays his hardest, scores points, concentrates on defense, and focuses on getting the ball to whomever has the best shot.

In the end, the star can score a career-high number of points and win accolades from the coach and fans, but if the team loses the game, that loss shows up on the star's record, too.

Likewise, if the health care organization that Sarah, John, Bob, and Grace work for has to shut down because it's losing money—money that the accounts payable department might have been able to recoup for the organization—each of the team members is still unemployed, no matter who had the best idea or did the most work on the project, *no matter who is to blame for the failure.*

So it doesn't matter who is to blame. It matters only that the problem is resolved, that the project is successful, that the organization stays open for business.

Every member of the team has to be *totally* responsible for the outcome before anyone knows what the outcome is.

If I am totally responsible for the outcome, though, that does not mean that I'm going to do your job for you. That is not responsible behavior on my part.

I'm not going to cover for you, pick up your slack, or keep you from getting into trouble with the boss. I'm not going to *rescue* you, *fix* you, or *save* you.

Likewise, if I am 100 percent responsible, that doesn't mean I have to boss everyone around or do everything myself. That is not responsible behavior, either.

If each team member has agreed to be responsible for the outcome of the project, then, what happens when one of the members falls short? Should the others pitch in and do her work for her?

No!

Instead, responsible team members confront their colleague, revisit the clear expectations that they all agreed to at the outset, and ask for her renewed commitment.

This isn't always easy to do, but the results of such a confrontation are often surprising.

Perhaps she is slacking, for example, not because she is lazy or irresponsible, but because she is ill or has a personal problem that her coworkers didn't know about.

If that's the case, they can ask her, "What do you need to do and what do we need to do to accommodate your needs while still getting this work done?"

A team works together to work things out. When they need help working things out, they enlist the help of their manager.

That's a far more efficient strategy than talking behind the "slacker's" back, jumping to conclusions, or working overtime to cover up for her or failing to finish the project successfully.

A true team exposes underperformance immediately. It gets it out into the open and deals with it—and it doesn't tolerate it.

Why? Each member of the team owns the success of the project—100 percent of it—so nobody wants it to fail. The life or death of the project depends on each individual contribution from team members.

In a surgical suite, for example, where each doctor, nurse and technician has a specific, distinct job and role that is different from everyone else's, each member of that team has the same goal: to successfully complete the operation without harming the patient.

If one person is not doing her job, the others know it immediately and snap her to it right away. If they are not responsible for doing that, the patient could die.

A dead patient will remain on the conscience of every person in that room, not just the one who slipped up.

Being 100 percent responsible for the success of a team effort is a challenge for each team member. It does not make you responsible for another person.

It means you need to take action—immediate action—if there's a breakdown because another team member is slipping up.

Don't wait for the manager or for another team member to intervene. You are responsible.

Say: *Here is what we agreed to. Here is what we need to do to get this done.*

The teammate might tell you to jump in a lake; that is a risk you take.

But you take a greater risk if you say nothing: You risk that the team member will continue to slip (remember, behavior that is rewarded is repeated) and that the team's effort will fail.

Follow the Leader?

Just as each member of a team is 100 percent responsible for the outcome of the effort, so is the person who assigned it.

If a busy working mother promises to bake a cake for the church bake sale but assigns it instead to her thirteen-year-old daughter, who agrees to the task but burns the cake, who is responsible for not getting the cake to the sale?

Who is responsible when an elderly parent falls ill from poor nutrition when his three adult children each leave it to the others to drive him to the grocery store on Saturdays?

Is the mother or the father responsible when a child plays video games instead of doing her homework and fails a class? Or is the child responsible?

Here are two answers to all of those questions:

1. All of the above are responsible—totally and equally.
2. Who cares whose fault it is when the outcome is unwanted?

Finding fault doesn't get the cake to the bake sale, the man to the grocery store, or the kid into college. It just gives us something to talk about. It lets me be right if I say you're wrong.

At least in my own mind.

If a team isn't getting the job done, does blaming one of the members resolve the problem?

Can a manager at work use these excuses to absolve himself of responsibility for the outcome: *I inherited these people . . . They put me in this position . . . I can't talk to them . . . They messed it up . . . It's not my fault!*

This is more honest: *I am unwilling to talk to them . . . I find them hard to talk to, and I'm not going to pretend otherwise . . . I take total responsibility for my decision not to talk to them . . . I am responsible for the outcome of this project, good or bad.*

A leader—the working mom, the adult children, the parents, or the manager—is just as responsible as the team is for the outcome of any project undertaken by that team.

The boss who doesn't stand up and accept the responsibility he or she had all along, the one who lays blame on his or her subordinates for the failures of the department or the company, is a weak boss, unlikely to win respect—or their best work—from employees.

The parent who blames her children for not doing what she told them to is an ineffective parent. Both are responsible.

How effective are you?

Look at your kids, your marriage, your employees, your coworkers. Are they and their efforts—which you participate in or oversee or at least influence—successful?

It's up to you to decide how effective you are. You are responsible for your level of effectiveness.

Responsibility is a mind-set that results in confidence, success, influence, and happiness, and it is the first prong of the 85% Solution.

How responsible are you? You can reveal your level of responsibility by honestly answering the questionnaire in the next chapter.

The Accountability Quotient, Part 1

Personal responsibility is a "before-the-fact" mind-set of personal ownership and commitment to a result.

How responsible are you for your own choices, behaviors, and actions—before you know how everything will turn out? In this chapter, you can measure your level of personal responsibility.

On *Exhibit 1,* use a scale from zero to 5 (zero is "none" and 5 is "100 percent") to rate your own sense of ownership, or responsibility, for each action you take. (The guidelines following the table will help you interpret your result.)

EXHIBIT 1. Your Responsibility Quotient

Category	Best Possible	Accumulated Score
Responsibility		*50*
Questions	*Rating Distribution*	

1. I am totally responsible for my success at work.	0	1	2	3	4	5
2. I make sure I clarify what my customers expect of me on an ongoing basis by putting agreements in writing.	0	1	2	3	4	5
3. Before I begin a project, I plan for any possible difficulties that may occur.	0	1	2	3	4	5
4. I clearly understand the authority I have to do my job.	0	1	2	3	4	5
5. I am exceptionally skilled for the work I do.	0	1	2	3	4	5
6. When I hold coworkers accountable, they do not feel personally attacked.	0	1	2	3	4	5
7. I hold others accountable for their commitments, regardless of the consequences to me.	0	1	2	3	4	5
8. I believe working through in-depth interpersonal issues, when necessary, is crucial to the success of the organization.	0	1	2	3	4	5

(Continued)

EXHIBIT 1. *(Continued)*

Category	Best Possible	Accumulated Score
Responsibility	*50*	
Questions	*Rating Distribution*	
9. I am provided timely feedback on my job performance.	0 1 2 3 4 5	
10. I am provided with information needed to understand the big picture.	0 1 2 3 4 5	

INTERPRET YOUR SCORE

High

If your responses add up to 40 or more, you are living the 85% Solution! Your score indicates a high level of responsibility. You accept 80 percent to 100 percent responsibility for your own choices, behaviors, and outcomes.

Your score indicates that a responsibility mind-set is an integral part of how you already approach the work you do and your role in life. Here are claims you can make with confidence on your performance evaluation or on your résumé:

- I know my professional definition of success. In fact, I've written it down and use it as a living document. I own my success and keep up with redefining it as circumstances and the environment change.

- I make clear agreements—in writing. I know clear agreements create trust and the basis for holding myself and others accountable up front.
- I understand the vital distinction between having "authority" and "being empowered."
- I am a student of my interpersonal skills and consistently seek to improve them.
- I am committed to understanding the big picture and owning my role in accomplishing the goals of the organization.

Medium

If your responses add up to between 30 and 40, your score indicates that you have the potential to adopt a responsibility mind-set that can change your life and guarantee your success. You accept between 60 percent and 70 percent responsibility for your own choices, behaviors, and outcomes.

If you are willing to look at and own your role in what is not working in your life, and if you have the will to change, you can live the 85% Solution. Here are some tasks to move you toward that goal:

- Work with a coach to write a professional definition of success that will serve as a living document for you. This will begin your journey to owning your success. It is critical that you keep up with redefining your success as circumstances and the environment change.
- Require clear, written agreements with teammates and bosses so you are responsible for having clear expectations

and an understanding of what is expected of you. Clear agreements also eliminate the potential for excuses and blame because someone was not clear with you.

- Write down your understanding of your role and authority to carry out each task or project and check it out with your boss or team. Be open to feedback.
- Ask three people you trust how you can improve your interpersonal skills. Summarize their responses in a performance improvement plan.

Low

If your responses add up to less than 30, your score indicates that you are adrift about who you are and what you want. You accept less than half of the responsibility for your own successes or failures.

It's time to take a hard look at your role in creating the situation you are in now and make some decisions. If the way things are going now is working for you, no change is needed. But if you want new scenery in your life, define what it is that you want—and get moving.

Don't fool yourself about being able to go it alone. Take these first small steps toward the 85% Solution:

- Invite someone into your life to work with you daily until you have a written list of achievable goals.
- Ask three people you trust how you can improve your interpersonal skills and summarize the responses.
- Take classes that address the areas you have been provided feedback on.

PART II

Self-Empowerment

Make a Splash

At four years old, my daughter Lea was a powerful little girl—powerful enough to change her life forever simply by jumping off the side of a swimming pool and into the water for the first time.

I had urged her to go for it, of course, because it would be fun, and simply because she could do it, because the water wasn't very deep.

Still, she wouldn't jump. I knew—and at age four, even she knew—that those things weren't for me to decide.

Oh, she wanted to jump in.

She envied the other kids who were showing off their cannonballs and belly flops, splashing everyone around them, then laughing, pointing at each other and climbing back out of the pool, puffing up their proud chests and rushing into the water again and again.

She wanted to be like those kids, to have all that fun, too, but she had never jumped into the water before and was afraid she would get water up her nose, wind up with soaking wet hair, or worse, wind up in water over her head with no way out.

Nothing I could say could alleviate those fears for her. She had to find out for herself.

Likewise, nothing I said could help her make her decision.

I'm a big, tall grown-up who can hold my breath for minutes at a time. She was just four and had barely ever put her nose under the water. My sense of how easy this was had no bearing on how she perceived the task at hand.

She had to gauge the risks for her four-year-old self and decide whether she could beat them or at least whether it would be worth it to inhale a noseful of pool water if she couldn't.

It was enlightening to witness her mind at work. She set it on making a plan.

First, she figured out how to mitigate the risks: She would jump only a few inches from the side of the pool instead of way out into the middle like the bigger kids; and she would ask me—someone she trusted—to stand right below her so I could catch her before any water found its way into her nostrils.

She directed me to stand a little closer to her, and when I refused to budge, she clamped her toes onto the pool's edge, leaned forward, and stretched out her arms to determine if her tiny body could close the gap between us.

Again, I explained that jumping in meant letting go of the side of the pool.

Then she presented me with one condition: I was to catch her before any water got in her nose or her hair got wet. I agreed. She considered. We talked about it. Minutes went by.

Then she jumped.

I caught her, dry hair and nose intact. She giggled. For her, it was so worth the risk. And immediately she said, "Let's do it again!"

And she did. But this time, she told me to back away farther. The thrill of the first leap had made my little swimmer eager to do more, to do better. I was watching her grow and learn and expand, all with one jump into the pool.

It was Lea's show. She made a choice, figured out how to get what she wanted (fun) without getting stuck with what she didn't (water up her nose), enlisted the aid of someone she trusted, and took the leap.

She asked for help. That's something full-grown executives have a hard time admitting they need.

She empowered herself.

Someone who observed the scene might say that I empowered her by patiently taking her through the steps she came up with and agreeing to catch her.

I didn't. It was Lea's idea to enlist me as her safety net.

She's the one who had to decide whether she could trust me to keep my pledge that I wouldn't let her hair get wet and whether I was strong enough physically to catch her before her face slipped under the water.

She's the one who had to decide whether it would be worth it to get her hair wet if I fell short.

She's the one who had to decide whether the potential for great fun outweighed the potential for a snout full of chlorine.

In the end, satisfied that she was more likely to have fun than to suffer, even if her hair did get wet, she jumped.

She took the risks and the action she needed to take in order to get what she wanted.

She empowered herself.

Empower Thyself

*E*mpowerment is the act of living life.

It's what you do. It's taking action and facing risk in order to get what you want. It's the way to ensure that you achieve a result.

Self-empowerment is the second of three critical steps that are part of every successful project or relationship. I discussed the first step, personal responsibility, in Part I. I delve into the third and final step, personal accountability, in Part III.

Empower yourself to succeed. Take the actions—and take the risks—that you need to in order to ensure that you achieve the results you want.

The three pieces of the 85% Solution—personal responsibility, self-empowerment, and accountability—are inseparable. You can't have empowerment without personal responsibility and personal accountability.

Empowerment involves a mind-set of ownership and personal responsibility, a mind-set that something needs to be different, and a mind-set that you're going to do what you have to in order to make it different.

(I don't want to sit on the side of the pool and watch the other kids have all the fun. I want to jump in. How can I make that happen?)

I'm going to empower myself, take an action, accept the risk, make it happen—and then answer for the result.

There is only one person who can empower you, and that's you.

There is only one kind of empowerment, and that's self-empowerment.

An empowered person takes risks. You can empower yourself by living by these mantras:

- Realize that my results are the consequences of my choices.
- If it is to be, it's up to me.
- Step out of my comfort zone.
- Keep focused.

Do you spend too much time sitting in your chair, watching too much TV, eating too many potato chips, talking only about "comfortable" topics, avoiding challenges, and staying the same year after year?

Why?

It could be that you, like so many people, have a misguided belief that someone else has to empower you to get up off your behind and make something of your life.

It could be that you blame others for your own status quo.

It could be that you're sitting and waiting for someone to bonk you on the head and empower you.

You're going to be waiting for a long, long time. It will never happen.

Here's what will happen if you believe someone else can empower you: You will give that person power over you. You will make yourself his victim.

Why in the world would you choose to assign responsibility for your success and well-being to someone else?

Perhaps you need someone to blame for your failures and shortcomings.

I could have been a supervisor, but my company only promotes women. (My company is responsible for my success. I'm just a victim.)

I'm a better technician than Frank is, but he got promoted because the boss likes him better. (The boss is responsible for my success. He won't empower me.)

The only reason she got the job is because she plays in a charity golf tournament with the CEO every spring. (My competitor is responsible for my success. There's nothing I can do about her.)

Have you considered that perhaps the women being promoted are working extra hard in order to win those plum jobs, or that the boss likes Frank better because he frequently approaches him with good ideas about how to get the work done more efficiently, or that the golfer started signing up for tournaments so she would have access to company brass outside the office—and that might get her noticed?

In each case, the one who got the promotion was proactive about going after what he or she wanted.

If you were passed over, it's because you didn't empower yourself to succeed—and you believe it's somebody else's fault that you're stuck in the same dead-end job.

When you think about the things you want that you don't have, do you blame other people?

Do you feel someone else's success has hindered you from being successful?

Do you say to yourself and others, "It's not my fault"?

Are you waiting for someone to give you that one lucky break?

Give it to yourself. You have that ability. In fact, you're the only one who does.

It's true that others can create a positive, nurturing environment that makes it easy for someone to become self-empowered. It's equally true that others can contribute to a hostile environment that makes self-empowerment seem impossible.

It's possible to walk into a meeting, sit down at the dinner table, face someone during a negotiation, or even answer the phone and know immediately whether you're entering an environment that encourages or discourages empowerment.

Still, empowerment comes from within. A discouraging environment is one in which you have to work harder—and perhaps be smarter—in order to empower yourself and get the results you want.

If you find yourself in an environment that truly discourages self-empowerment and you discover you cannot thrive there, you can choose to change it—by confronting the boss about the negative atmosphere, for example, and suggesting ways to improve it—or to leave it—by looking for another job at a place that appreciates proactive employees.

You can empower yourself to create or find a better environment.

Sound scary? Create a safety net.

Remember Lea's big jump into the pool? She was able to justify the risks, in part because she believed she would land safely in my arms. If she hadn't felt that, she might still be sitting on the side of the pool watching the other kids have all the fun.

This is where the big hiccup happens in terms of understanding empowerment: It's used synonymously with "granting authority."

The two terms are not related.

You can grant someone authority to do something.

You cannot grant empowerment. Empowerment comes from within.

Consider the boss who says to a taxi driver, "I empower you to drive this eighteen-wheel truck."

The taxi driver has never even ridden in an eighteen-wheel truck, let alone driven one or applied for a license to drive one.

Still, his boss has empowered him to do it. Does that make him a truck driver?

It does not.

It means the boss has given him permission to drive it, has authorized him to drive it. But it doesn't mean he knows how or wants to or has a license to do so or will agree to do it.

No one can empower you with an ability to perform. That's within you. You show up with it.

Still, the taxi driver can empower himself.

He can ask his boss to clarify what he means: "Is the expectation that I drive this truck without knowing how?"

He can explain: "I need the authority to spend company funds to take driving lessons first, study the instruction manual and apply for my license."

If the boss says, "No," the driver can empower himself further: "I am unwilling to do it. I don't know how. It's not safe. Sorry, boss."

The taxi driver runs the risk that the boss will get angry or even fire him and hire someone who will agree to drive the truck; every choice involves a risk. Still, the driver has taken the risk to get what he wants: his own safety.

He knows he has taken charge of his own well-being rather than become a victim of his fears and of his boss. He's empowered.

He empowered himself.

The 85% Connection

If the story about the taxi driver in the previous chapter sounds familiar, it's because there is a one-to-one correlation between empowerment and responsibility.

The extent to which you are personally responsible is the extent to which you are empowered.

If you live at 100-zero—you believe that you are 100 percent responsible for your success and outside conditions have nothing to do with it—or if you take at least 85 percent of the responsibility for every outcome, you're not a person who makes excuses for your problems and failures or blames others.

It doesn't mean everything goes your way 100 percent of the time—nothing can guarantee that, of course—but at least the people who rely on you can predict how you will react when things don't work out.

They know you will be responsible for your choices and actions.

Responsibility is your mind-set before the fact; empowerment involves your actions in the here and now. It's the "doing it" part of the equation.

In order for you to be empowered—to self-empower—you need to be responsible.

In order to be responsible, you need to own your decisions fully.

In order to own your choices, you need to be clear about what you're choosing.

In order to be clear, you need to ask a lot of questions.

In fact, the most direct route to self-empowerment involves taking the risk to be clear about what you expect and about what is expected of you.

The source of all upset is a missed expectation—and there are no exceptions to that truism.

Yet it's risky to set or receive a set of clear expectations.

The risk is that if you are very clear about what you expect, someone might say, "If that's what you expect, I don't want to live/work/be with you. I don't like you or your list of expectations."

Or in the case of the taxi driver: "If you expect me to consider your safety before the job, I'll find someone who puts the job first."

Usually, our behavior is clearer than our words.

You might say to your spouse, "I really care about you." *But still, I'm seeing somebody else behind your back.*

Or to your boss: "I'm too sick to work today." *Still, it's the first warm day in a while, so I'm going to play golf.*

Or to your employees: "People are our most important resource." *But I will cut your job before I will cut my own pay.*

Those are lies.

What if somebody were to overhear you saying you are too sick to work and later saw you teeing off on the first hole? What would that do to your reputation?

If you're the boss and you're the one telling the lie, what would that do to staff morale? Maybe your employees will reason that if you're willing to lie about being sick so you can enjoy the nice weather, you won't mind if they do it, too.

Instead, the empowered person says, "It's the first nice day we've had in a while, and I'd like to spend it playing golf. I will take a vacation day today."

That person is responsible for his choices and actions.

That person is taking a risk, too. The boss might say, "No."

But at least you're empowering yourself to be honest—just as you have empowered yourself to lie so many times. At least you're owning your choice. You're setting an example for people who work for you.

You can only teach at home or at work by example: by empowering yourself to set your choices into action, and by owning those choices and actions.

What's Your Point?

Suppose you're working with someone to whom being right is more important than being effective. The two of you hit a snag, and the project you've put your heads together on stalls.

Your partner says, "You shouldn't have done that."

You apply the 85% Solution. You have decided, before knowing the outcome, that you are responsible for the outcome of your choices and actions, good or bad.

You reply, "You're right. I shouldn't have done that. Let's do it another way and fix the problem."

Your partner persists, "Now we have to start over. That was stupid."

Don't punch. Don't yell. Don't fume.

Shut him up with one question, "What's your point?"

The fact is, he doesn't have a point. He lives on Planet Guilt.

He needs to be right, which means he has to prove that you are wrong. That's more important to him than getting the project back on track.

You ask, "Do you need to be right even if that means we don't get our work done?"

If the answer seems to be "Yes," you have three choices: First, you can waste your time arguing with your partner over who is right. Second, you can concede the point. Or, third, you can empower yourself not to work with that person.

Tell your partner that the arrangement is not going to work out, and then tell it to the boss. Come up with an alternative plan so that the work will get done.

Don't waste your day with someone who's going to sabotage your success or add to your stress.

Walk away.

BULLY FOR YOU

Walk away is what my client Melissa did—after a long, torturous ordeal with a bully in her office named Ed.

Melissa was a department director at a fairly large company. Ed, also a director, publicly badgered her.

For reasons Melissa did not understand, her boss always stood up for Ed. So it took a lot of courage for her to ask the boss for help.

His response? "Meet with Ed and work it out."

Melissa considered it. She knew Ed only picked on individuals who were nonconfrontational and would not challenge him when he was out of line. This included the boss, a man who actively avoided confrontation.

In addition, Ed isolated others, including those he feared, talking about them behind their backs in an effort to discredit them and make himself look better.

After making that mental list, Melissa realized she would not be able to "work it out" with Ed. When she had challenges with other colleagues, she was able to resolve them because the other individual wanted that, too. Agreements happen only when both parties are willing to find ways to work things out.

In this case, Melissa knew Ed felt threatened by her knowledge and ability and would never believe that all she wanted to do was work well together.

Adding it all up, Melissa came to the conclusion she was being bullied by Ed, and that her boss was not going to take kindly to that observation.

Putting a bully and his target—Melissa—in the same room to "work it out"—even with a neutral party to mediate—wasn't going to work, she concluded.

Together, Melissa and I came up with a plan for dealing with this bully.

First, she recognized Ed for the bully he is, and understood that it was appropriate for her to ask her boss to intervene.

Second, she took some time off from work so she could make a clear-headed decision about whether she should continue working for a boss who would not address her very important concern.

Finally, she thought about the kinds of coping mechanisms she could employ that would help her deal with Ed if she decided to stay at that organization. For example, she would never meet with him alone and would document all of their conversations.

Melissa decided she did not want to continue to work with Ed or for her boss. In fact, she wonders why it took her so long to realize it.

Melissa knows there may be more bullies in her future, but she's ready for them.

Her armor: She knows she alone is responsible for her success and for her reaction to others. That's a great protection against putting up with a job where bullies hang out.

The Choice Is Yours

Most people can empower themselves most of the time, yet they don't.

Here's a typical conversation with one of my clients, who is waiting for someone else to empower her—something that will never, ever happen:

ME: Are you empowered to do that?
SHE: No.
ME: Why not?
SHE: I don't have the authority to do it.
ME: Go and get the authority.
SHE: I can't.

So far, it appears that my client is blaming her inability to complete her assignment on her lack of authority. So I press on:

ME: You can't, or you are unwilling to?

SHE: I won't.

ME: Why not?

SHE: Because they might give it to me.

ME: What's the problem with that?

SHE: If I have the authority to do this, then I'll have to answer for it. I don't want to.

I don't want to.

Nobody but she could empower her to complete her task. When she finally got honest about it, it became clear that she *chose* not to seek the authority she needed because she didn't really want it.

Nobody had denied her that authority.

Her startling admission didn't get the work done, but it was a responsible statement.

It was the statement of someone who finally empowered herself to admit that she did not want the authority or the responsibility for what she was being asked to do.

She finally admitted that she was in control of her own situation. She could no longer blame her boss or other outside conditions. She owned her choice.

Why are you saying you can't do that when you really just don't *want* to do it?

Ask for something you want? Tell someone she disappointed you? Finish a project that requires hard work?

The fact is, you can.

If you don't want to, or if you refuse to, or if you simply aren't going to, why not say so?

You'll save yourself and everyone involved the trouble of worrying about when and if and how you're going to do something that you know in your heart you will never get done.

In your heart, you have already chosen not to do it.

It's 100 percent responsible to say you won't if, indeed, you don't intend to.

It's not responsible to say you will if you really won't.

And saying you "can't" just isn't true. It's a lie you tell yourself—and everyone else—when you are unwilling to be responsible for your choice.

Saying, "I am unwilling" is true.

"I can't" is a lie that you hope will convince others that you have no choice—that someone or something besides you is to blame.

It might work at deflecting blame from you. But it won't get the work done, and it won't make you the hero. You'll still be the person who couldn't overcome whatever obstacle you blamed for your failure.

No matter why you say you failed to do it, you still failed to do it.

Is that the reputation you want?

Give yourself permission.

Everything you do every minute of the day is a choice.

You can choose whether you yell at someone who makes you angry or, instead, calmly ask the person to come back at another time so you can resolve your differences after you've settled down.

If you choose to scream at your colleague and call him a jerk, you've empowered yourself to behave that way.

You're responsible for what happens as a result. Perhaps you will ruin the working relationship, but you chose it.

Likewise, you can choose whether you put a task off until the last minute or devote your focus to it so it's done well and on time. If you put it off and hand in sloppy work, the consequences are still yours because the choice was yours.

In fact, plenty of people choose not to do jobs that might make them more successful in their careers.

Maybe you have a shot at a promotion but you don't go for it because the new job would require you to work more hours. Or make speeches, and you'd rather die than make a speech. Or travel more than you'd like. Or supervise your friends and you don't want to ruin your friendships.

Maybe you don't want the job because it will require you to work harder than you do now, and you really don't want to work that hard.

There's nothing wrong with making that choice if it's the right one for you.

Like my client, you might not want to be responsible for a project or you might not want to be held accountable for its success or failure. So you do not empower yourself to get the authority you need to do the work.

If that's the case, you can still empower yourself. Empower yourself to say "No."

What's wrong with saying, "This isn't for me. I'm happy with my status quo. I do not want any more responsibility. It doesn't make me happy."

That's a responsible statement, a responsible choice.

That's true not only at work but in your personal life.

How many times have you done something you didn't want to because your spouse wanted you to do it? Or because your friends or family said it would be the best thing for you?

How many of your friends are unhappily married to spouses their friends convinced them were "right" or have made a career in a field that doesn't interest them because their parents pushed them into it?

Those people are not self-empowered. If they were, they would have made different choices back then. They would change their circumstances by making different choices now.

Annie is seventy and has finally empowered herself to start living the life she always wanted.

As a teenager, Annie, a small-town Minnesota girl, longed to attend nursing school in St. Paul and live and work there after she graduated.

Her widowed mother wanted her only child to stay closer to home, about 60 miles from the city center. So Annie ditched school and got a job as a receptionist in the local obstetrician's office. She rarely visited St. Paul after that.

As she fantasized about the nightlife, the college-educated friends, the fast pace, and the job opportunities in the Twin Cities, she blamed her mother.

Before long, she married a neighborhood boy and started her family in the same small town where she grew up.

When her mother passed away years later, Annie approached her husband about moving to St. Paul. But he was happiest in his home town, so she chose to give up her dream for the sake of a harmonious household.

When the pangs of regret overtook her, she blamed her husband.

Then, her husband lost his factory job and got an offer from a bigger company in Minneapolis. Together, they decided it would be a bad time to pull their two adolescent children out of their tiny, familiar classrooms and thrust them into a school with hundreds of students much wiser in urban ways. It wasn't long before she was crying herself to sleep because the life she dreamed of was passing her by. She blamed her children.

Now she's retired, and she has run out of people to blame.

In fact, the small-town girl in Annie just never let go of the old neighborhood and the family, friends, memories, and safety that reside there with her. She could have defied her mother, convinced her husband, acclimated her children.

She chose not to. She was *afraid* to go.

She chose not to go, and she did everything in her power to stay.

She just never admitted it.

Until she retired and both of her kids moved to St. Paul. With nobody left to blame and an empty home that suddenly felt way too big for the two of them, Annie finally shared her dreams and her resentments with her husband.

He said he had been ready to move since he lost his old job years ago, but he knew she didn't really want to go.

Today, she lives with her husband in a sun-drenched St. Paul apartment and volunteers as a family liaison at the university hospital.

You're never too old to empower yourself to make your dreams come true.

Empowerment in Real Numbers

Here's another story of empowerment, this time from my client Andy T., the owner of a fuel company.

He told me this story of self-empowerment a few days after complaining that his financial people were questioning why he was spending so much time and money sending his employees to my seminars on personal accountability.

The accountant wanted to see "real numbers" to prove that the education was showing a return on the company's investment.

In tonight's episode, we join night fuel driver Jeff B., a notoriously helpless but lovable chap who seems to occupy limitless amounts of the fleet supervisor's time as he asks for help fixing every little thing that goes wrong with his truck in the middle of the night.

On this night, however, Jeff is remembering what he learned during Linda Galindo's seminar about adopting a 100-zero attitude and empowering himself to take the risks and actions he needs to get what he wants.

Jeff B., it seems, has taken those lessons to heart.

Let's join Jeff in the middle of his route somewhere in Fontana (affectionately referred to as "Fontucky" by the folks here, given its distance from the Salt Lake City headquarters) as he calls up Fleet Supervisor Chris T. at his house around 10:30 P.M.

CHRIS: (in pajamas, half asleep): Hello?

JEFF: Chris, it's Jeff. I know this is the last thing you probably want to hear, but I accidentally backed the truck into a pole and snapped off two of the air connections. The truck is losing so much air pressure that it's not safe to drive back to the plant.

CHRIS: (pauses to calculate the six hours of travel and repair time this will take him and the 20 times he's been through this before with Jeff) Damn it, Jeff. Okay, tell me where you are. It's going to take me a few hours to get to you.

JEFF: (a sudden look of enlightenment spreading across his face) Chris, you know what? The Peterbilt shop is just two miles away from me. The truck is safe to drive that far. If we had an account there I could take it there myself and just wait while they fixed it. I might even be able to finish my route!

CHRIS: (in total disbelief) We do have an account there, Jeff.

JEFF: Okay, I'm back in the truck. I'm going to take it there right now. You don't need to come out.

CHRIS: (reaching out to the bedpost to steady himself) Uh . . . okay, Jeff. You will call me when it's fixed and you are back on the road, right?

JEFF: Yes, I will.

(Jump ahead to 1:00 A.M., as the phone rings at Chris's house again.)

CHRIS: Hello?

JEFF: Chris, it's Jeff. The truck is fixed. I'm back on the road. I still have time to finish the route. Thanks for your help.

(Curtain lowers. Band plays ending fanfare.)

So a human being is learning to take charge of his own life, and another one is getting part of his life back. Plus, the new, self-empowered Jeff B. saved the company at least $200 in overtime, just for letting the supervisor stay in bed instead of driving to Fontana. He also saved another $100 or so by avoiding a call to another driver, who would have had to divert from his own route to cover the stops that Jeff B. would have missed.

Where is that accountant who asked me about "real numbers"? I've got something to show him.

Your Unique Definition of Success

How do people get stuck in small towns when they want to live in the big city? In careers their parents nudged them into? In dead-end jobs that bore them? In marriages they knew wouldn't last?

They don't know what they want, so they do what others want for them. Or they stay where they're comfortable because they don't know what they would do instead.

Know what you want before somebody knows it for you.

Decide what you want and write it down.

If you don't know what you want, you won't get it.

If you want success but you don't know what "success" means—exactly—you won't be successful.

You might have some successes, but they'll be inconsistent and accidental.

Take control of your success. Define what success means to you. Know what the "prize" is for you. Then go for it. This is critically important when everything around you is changing, like your job or your job security.

Just as you're the only one who can empower yourself to take the actions and risks that can make you successful, you're the only one who can define what success means to you.

Success can come in a million different packages.

Your definition of success might be far different from your spouse's or parents' or boss's or best friend's.

Your definition of career success might be far different from your definition of personal success.

If you don't map out your own definitions of success, they might conflict with each other.

Suppose you fantasize about being rich and you also dream of having a large family. So you have five kids and you accept a job that pays a bundle. All set?

Not quite. The job requires you to spend every Monday through Friday out of town. That means you can see your kids only on weekends, when you're exhausted from traveling.

Or is it that the kids require you to be in town, and that means you can't take the big job that you want?

Which is more important to you? What do you have to do in each case to feel successful—according to your unique definition of success?

Be honest. And be clear.

That kind of clarity can be scary.

What if your definition of success revolves around wealth and work, and not around your kids?

Own it.

"Success" isn't how you react to circumstances. It's what you want and need to feel fulfilled, happy, and worthwhile.

What do you want and need?

Think about the things you've done with passion and dedication. Most often, they turned out just as you had hoped—or even better.

That's because you knew what you wanted, and you went for it.

You empowered yourself to do what you had to do—to take the risks and actions necessary—to achieve your goal. Your first step was to determine what you wanted. Where did you hope your actions would take you? In this way, you created a definition of success for yourself.

Defining *success* is the best way to get some focus in your life.

It's a personal statement about the future you want—as of now. It's a brief, to-the-point outline of what it means to you to be successful.

Does your success rely on how much money you make? How many countries you visit? How often you eat dinner with your family?

Write it down. Look at it every morning. Live it.

My own personal definition of success comprises the four most important components of my life: my family, my work, my health, and my involvement in my community. So I have a four-part definition of success.

Here it is:

1. *My definitions for professional success:*
   - I am doing work I love with creative, evolved individuals who love the adventure of life.

- I speak and write on the topic I love.
- I spend no more than six nights a month away from my family.

2. *My definitions for home success:*
   - I have dinner with my family four nights a week.
   - I go out on "dates" with my husband at least twice a month.
   - I am able to leave work at the office and concentrate on my family.

3. *My definitions for health success:*
   - I maintain a certain weight.
   - I exercise at least four times per week for 30 minutes.

4. *My definition for community success:*
   - I get and respond to regular feedback from my peers about my performance on the boards of directors that I choose to serve on.

It's a business risk to limit my travel to six nights a month, but when I do it, I am tremendously successful. I was most miserable—and least successful—when I said I would do this and was gone all of the time.

My definitions of success are in line with my priorities, and it's my priority to be available to my children.

Likewise, it's important to me—and to my family—that I come home from work in a frame of mind that allows me to pay attention to our home life.

If I'm stressed and angry when I arrive at home, I'm horrible to be around. I act like it's not my fault I'm in a bad mood. I blame outside conditions.

Yes, I fall off of my "I am 100 percent responsible" pedestal occasionally.

Very occasionally.

But I hop right back on. When it happens, I revisit my definitions of success and recommit to achieving success in all four areas of my life.

And I do treat those definitions as a commitment—to myself.

There have been times, for example, when I felt I wasn't receiving the feedback I asked for from the community groups to which I donated my time—and I resigned from the ones that fell short.

It's important to me to know that my contribution is making a difference—that I'm not wasting my time, because my time is precious to me—so I empowered myself to be selective about my participation on boards.

You can create a definition of success for yourself.

Turn off the TV and the Internet, put down the magazines and newspapers, and stop listening to everyone who pretends to know better than you do how to live your life.

Start listening to *you.*

Ask yourself: *If money were not an issue, what would I do?*

Think about the people who claim that if they won the lottery, they would continue to work. Why would they?

It's their human potential pushing from the inside to get out. Success to them means more than being rich.

What does it mean to you?

Your definition of success can be very specific or very broad.

One of my very successful colleagues defines *success* simply as "feeling at peace." That has powerful meaning to her and influences every decision she makes and every action she takes.

Last year, she declined to take on a project that would have doubled her income because the client treated her disrespectfully. Dealing with him, she decided, would have created discord: arguments, suspicion, uncertainty, bruised egos—the opposite of peaceful feelings.

Money under those circumstances does not contribute to her success. Her definition of success isn't about money alone.

My mother defines *success* as "solving problems."

Once I realized that, we started getting along better.

I had been telling her about my successes but chose not to burden her with my troubles, and it was hard for her to relate to me. Now that I know her definition of success, it works to reveal my problems to her, and we have plenty to talk about.

Whatever your definition of success, it will have three important qualities:

1. It is written. Do not store it in your head. Commit it to paper. Work on it. Refine it. Keep it someplace where you will see it every day.
2. It is stated in the "now," so it is achievable right now in your day-to-day life.
3. It segments the many roles you have in life: employee, spouse/parent, community volunteer—whatever is important to you.

Success is the conscious creation of what you want in life, but it's not a single goal. It's not something you can achieve and be done with. It's an ongoing commitment, an ongoing state of being.

Your definition of success aligns you with your goals, and it guides your day-to-day and moment-to-moment living.

When I am out of alignment with my definition of success, I am not successful. Nobody has to tell me what to do to get back on track. I already know. I wrote it down.

It's entirely up to me whether I do the things I need to do to achieve success as I have defined it. I own it fully.

Read your definition of success twice a day—when you wake up and before you go to bed. Always have it handy.

It is self-empowering to take the actions and risks that are necessary to achieve the outcomes you desire.

And those desires might change as your life changes.

You might define success differently when you're in your twenties and single than when you're in your forties and have a family.

Whenever you redefine success, recommit yourself to be totally responsible for achieving that success.

EXHIBIT 2. Examples of Professional Definitions of Success

When I am successful:

Consultant

- I am solution oriented and committed to customer and coworker success.
- I realize professional income of $XXXX per year.
- I do not travel more than six nights per month.
- I work with colleagues who are high energy and have clarity about their own work.

College Instructor

- I inspire students to want to learn.
- I teach one new class each year.
- I participate in Toastmasters weekly.

Corporate Director

- I mentor and coach and I spend one-quarter of my time at work working on strategic planning.
- I manage staff at the level they need.
- I hold others accountable for their agreements with me.

EXHIBIT 3. Developing Your Professional Definition of Success

Step 1: As you craft your own unique definition of success, think about your answers to these questions:

1. What about your current job or role provides the most satisfaction?
2. What about your current job or role makes you feel successful?
3. What set of conditions do you need to create an atmosphere that lets you thrive?
4. What support would you need to create a situation where the conditions you attribute to success are present?

Step 2: Based on your answers to these four questions, write statements that represent your professional definition of success.

#1: I _____

#2: I _____

#3: I _____

#4: I _____

Spread the Word

My former assistant wanted to be a consultant and a coach like I am. I knew I was not going to change her role in my organization so that she could do that.

Her role—which I clearly outlined in her position description—was to run the office, keep my schedule straight, and help my staff of consultants and coaches with everything from hotel reservations to research.

But she would never do what we do for a living—at least not as long as she worked for me. She simply was not qualified for the specific kind of work that the consultants in my company do.

When I work with others, I ask each of them to share their definition of success with me. Once I know how someone defines success, I can be supportive as he or she works toward achieving it.

The former assistant defined success as becoming a professional equal to the consultants and coaches she assisted. Once I learned that, I told her that my company was not the place for her.

I offered to help her find a job with a consulting firm that could elevate her to a position that offered this opportunity. I didn't want to keep her from realizing success as she defined it.

I wasn't trying to be mean; in fact, I really like this assistant. If she could be successful working as an assistant in my consulting firm, I would have encouraged her to stay with me forever.

I didn't tell her she would never be a consultant and coach. I told her she wouldn't be one in my company. She had written a definition of success that was not possible for her to achieve if she chose not to change companies.

So I helped her move on to a job that's more suited to her definition of success.

That honest communication between us was hard on both of us. I take no pleasure in bursting someone's bubble—especially someone I like. She sobbed when she learned she would not be able to realize her goal as long as she worked for me.

Still, sharing her definition of success with me might save her years of working toward something that isn't available to her. Now she has the information she needs to make a good decision about whether to stay with my company or go to another one where she can achieve success as a consultant and coach.

Once you write your definition of success, share it with the people who can help you achieve it.

Are you afraid to do that?

Afraid someone like me will tell you that it's not possible for you to achieve success as you define it if you remain in the comfortable job, relationship, or situation you're used to?

That might happen. Spreading the word that you're responsible for your own success could mean you have to make some changes—and that others will push you to make those changes.

It's like telling your friends you quit smoking. The next time you light up, they're going to give you grief.

They'll also remind you of the reasons you gave them for your decision to quit. They'll encourage you, talk you through it, and buy you chewing gum. They'll hold you accountable for going back on your resolve.

They will do whatever they can to help you achieve your goal.

Sharing that life-changing decision with others is a huge step toward being 100 percent responsible for successfully kicking the habit. Being responsible for your success is your best chance for achieving it.

Likewise, sharing your definition of success with others is the best way to be responsible for achieving it.

Still reluctant? Ask yourself why.

Aren't you clear about what success means to you?

Get clear. You will not achieve success if you don't know what "success" is.

Aren't you willing to do what it takes—to make the changes necessary—to achieve your vision of success?

Then rewrite your definition. Write: *Success is being comfortable and not having to challenge myself by changing or taking risks.*

It's okay with me if it's okay with you.

As long as you're honest about it. As long as you *own* it.

As long as you never say someone else prevented you from succeeding. This is a decision you make on your own.

If you are willing to take the risks you need to achieve what you want, say so—out loud.

Make it public—at least among the people you trust—and make it real.

Brace yourself, and share your definition of success with your spouse, your boss, your friends, and your colleagues. Their feedback will help you determine whether you can be successful as you define it while you remain in your current job and your current relationships.

Plus, they'll be in a better position to support you if they know what it means to you.

And they might realize that your definition of success is different from theirs. Maybe they'll stop pushing you to have children if they know you don't want them, or to quit your job if they know it makes you successful.

I'd like to see all engaged couples—both fiancé and fiancée—write a definition of success for their lives, their careers, and their marriages—and share it with each other before they walk down the aisle.

HIS: Success is quitting my high-powered, high-paying job and writing poetry full time.

HERS: Success is having a high-powered, high-earning husband who buys me a summer home in the Hamptons and a Mercedes to park in my three-car garage.

Oops! Or:

HIS: Success is having a large family and enough money so my wife can stay home full-time with the children.

HERS: Success is being a partner at my law firm by the time I'm 35 and trying the highest-profile cases, even if I have to work 60 hours a week to do it and delay starting a family until I'm in my forties.

Do these two know *anything* about each other?

In both cases, at least one of the partners—and probably both—will be unable to achieve success in the relationship. Wouldn't you like to know if the person you're about to marry will never feel successful unless you change *your* definition of success? Or that *you* will never feel successful unless your partner's definition changes?

A prenuptial "definition disclosure" might stymie the divorce rate by parting a few mismatched pairs.

Don't apologize for defining success as you envision it for yourself, even if you come up with a definition that's different than people expect. *Do* let the people you care about know how you define success so they can help you rather than unintentionally stand in your way.

Go for the Goal

Live your definition of success right now.

Once you define success for yourself, empower yourself to go for it! The trick is to focus on the outcome you desire.

To borrow a powerful phrase from the civil rights movement: Keep your eyes on the prize.

There is a distinct difference between people who consider themselves successful and those who do not: Successful people are focused, and unsuccessful people are not.

Knowing what your life is about adds stability, balance, and direction to it.

A lack of focus causes problems. Which of the following categories best describes you?

- I have written goals, complete with action plans that I revise periodically.

- I think about what I want, and I do not need to write out my goals.
- I am comfortable being unclear about what I want. Goal setting is too restrictive, and life would be boring if I were that disciplined.
- I feel I have enough to handle, doing my job, taking care of my children or parents—or both—and all the other things in my life. Writing goals is a useless exercise.

Confronting a blank piece of paper with pen in hand, poised to write out a personal vision or goals, can be intimidating.

Do it anyway. The results can be astonishing.

Face it. Force it if you have to. Do it.

You'll reap measurable benefits almost immediately.

Keep living with nothing in particular and everything in general in mind, and that's exactly what will continue to show up.

That's perfectly acceptable if you're comfortable that way. It's okay with me if you're not successful, as long as it's okay with you.

As long as you own it.

As long as you know it's your choice, and nobody's fault.

If you'd rather be more successful than you are, focusing on your specific definition of success could make your world right.

Right now.

That's key to defining and understanding what success means to you. What is your vision for your most successful life right now?

This is where we get into that murky business of vision versus goals.

There's a difference between your vision for yourself and your goals.

Developing an overall vision for your life helps you see clearly into your future. Your vision may change as time goes on.

When Shelly was eight years old, she wanted to be a ballerina or a nun when she grew up. That was her genuine vision of her future at the time, albeit through adolescent eyes.

By the time she was in high school, she had decided that nursing or publishing were more up her alley.

But in college, she developed an interest in animals and studied veterinary medicine. After graduation, she opened her own practice.

Eight years later, she sold her practice and became a stay-at-home mom with three kids and four cats. Once the children were old enough for school, she went back to school herself and is working toward a PhD in literature. She's toying with a career change—maybe teaching.

At each stage of her life, Shelly's vision for herself, her success, and her future changed.

As your life and priorities change, so will your vision.

Whatever your vision is *right now*, set goals within that context. The goals are markers, but do not in themselves indicate success. Success is achieved in the moment, because as you live life *right now*, you create in each day what you want for yourself, and you enjoy immediate successes.

Most people who say they're successful can also show you a written list of their goals.

They can articulate their vision for themselves.

They can define what success means to them.

People who enjoy success also enjoy the challenge of moving toward fulfilling the goals on their list.

Even during times of chaos and crisis, those goals remain as beacons, a centering point for balance or redirection once the crisis passes.

People with focus—via their goals—happen to life. People without focus experience life happening to them.

Do you happen to life? Or do you watch passively as it happens to you—and as other people enjoy the successes you crave for yourself?

Empower yourself to choose.

Then go for it.

The next three chapters introduce ten self-empowering strategies that will help you accept 100 percent of the responsibility for your choices and actions. In them, I will show you how to empower your attitude, your words, and the way you spend your time, and how to embrace the success that follows.

Empower Your Attitude

You empower yourself to make an impression on other people. If they find you stand-offish, perhaps that's how you're choosing to behave. If they accuse you of being too busy for them, look at whether you're choosing to spend your time doing other things. If they ignore you, why are you letting them?

It's up to you. The three self-empowering strategies in this chapter will help you examine your choice to behave the way you do with other people, to determine whether you like the result, and to change your attitude and actions if you want to.

SELF-EMPOWERMENT STRATEGY #1: LIGHTEN UP

Darlene is the first to admit that she's a deeply serious person. Even when everything is absolutely fantastic, top-of-the-world incredible, she is serious.

Throw into that a little, "I don't deserve how great everything is," and, "If you're on a high, keep your guard up because the low is just around the corner," and you've got *serious.*

A manager who supervises dozens of employees at work, she didn't know that being so serious all the time could pose a problem for her or for her staff.

Her peers and subordinates routinely tell her to "lighten up."

They depend on Darlene to create an atmosphere that motivates them to come together to accomplish great and wonderful things. They want Darlene to be genuinely "up" and "into it" all of the time.

Unreasonable? Not really. Taking a job as a manager means that your attitude affects everyone else's.

So should Darlene slap on a stupid smile and grin at everyone all day? Jump up and down with excited praise when people do what they are paid to do?

Yes.

Sometimes you have to make yourself act happy or as if you are having fun until you begin to believe that you are.

It's a way to force yourself to stop what you have always done before.

If you excuse your behavior with, "That's just the way I am, and if people don't like it that's their problem," you'll probably have a hard time getting along with employees, bosses, colleagues, and even your own family.

Here's another example: Edwin travels often in his job. Although he enjoys traveling, the stress of being home just two days and then gone for a week takes its toll on workplace relationships.

He's always in a hurry and pressed to finish his urgent business before he takes off on another trip.

The casualties: his staff and colleagues at work, and his wife and children at home.

He has so little time or patience for casual "bonding" with the staff that they don't feel they know him. They don't feel he cares about them.

Let's not even talk about how neglected his family feels.

Edwin feels his colleagues and family should understand how pressed for time he is and excuse his abruptness or preoccupation with other matters.

They don't.

They don't have the same demanding schedules. So they don't have any real empathy for him. If he continues to expect them to understand, he will continue to upset them.

Like it or not, Edwin needs to schedule some down time between trips so he can get in the right frame of mind to interact with others while he is in the office and at home.

In the long run, it is not worth the stress to himself and others for Edwin to sacrifice these relationships in order to keep up a superhuman pace.

Getting into a frame of mind that helps you "lighten up" can be simple. Some strategies for success include

- Listening to positive messages or upbeat music before you go to work rather than focusing on depressing newscasts.

- Reading a daily affirmation from any best-selling inspirational book.
- Writing your own affirmation each morning. Write it several times.
- Visualizing the kind of workday you would like to have rather than dreading a bad day.

I learned this strategy during a golf lesson. My instructor asked me to name the golf club I most disliked. I admitted that I love my 5-iron but not the woods. When I use the woods, I explained, I always hit the ball at the wrong angle and wind up topping the ball so it barely moves. I "duff" it.

So he lined me up for a shot with my 1-wood—the driver. Just as I was going to swing, he shouted, "Stop! What are you thinking right now?"

"I'm thinking, 'Don't "duff" the shot!'" I admitted.

"That's the problem," he told me. "Your mind is registering only a missed shot. It wasn't hearing the *don't* part of 'Don't "duff" the shot.'"

He was right. I was seeing myself scraping the top of the ball with the wood instead of hitting it dead center as I should.

So he challenged me to change my thinking.

"See yourself taking a clear and powerful swing that connects with the ball," he instructed me.

I did. That ball went soaring!

Changing my thinking absolutely worked.

I use that concept every day. You can, too.

When you're facing a difficult meeting, a stressful confrontation with your family, or an extremely busy day, steer your thoughts toward the positive. Think about what you want, not what you don't want.

Smile, or—at the very least—don't frown. Your positive attitude will set the tone for your day. It will feed on itself.

These strategies sound simple. But for a manager like serious Darlene, they are anything but.

Still, she has resolved that once a week she will make a deliberate attempt to "lighten up."

If it doesn't work, she hasn't lost anything. If things improve, she will have learned something.

After that, she has to decide: She can keep using what she has learned or she can step back into the dark. It's her choice.

You have a choice, too.

SELF-EMPOWERMENT STRATEGY #2: WHAT'S DONE IS DONE

Mary arrives at a big meeting so excited about her tremendous idea that she's uncharacteristically enthusiastic and happy, despite her reputation for acting dour.

When it's her turn to describe her idea, someone cuts her off midway: "Not going to happen," the someone says, "but thanks for sharing."

Mary eyes the offender as if he has just killed her puppy, her cute, fluffy, drooling bundle of love.

She leaves the meeting, but not before she puts an imaginary leash on the lifeless, invisible puppy and drags it out of the room behind her.

A few people who attended the meeting and even some who didn't quickly become aware of the dead puppy.

Mary makes sure of it.

She tells everyone about the offender who killed her puppy. She defends her right to hold a grudge forever.

A year later, Mary goes to another meeting.

She plops the poor, dead puppy onto the middle of the table. A startled newcomer whispers to a colleague, "What's that?"

"Shhh," the coworker cautions. "It's Mary's dead puppy, and it's a sore subject. We don't talk about it."

To the newcomer, this is just weird. She doesn't understand why nobody is addressing the fact that there is a dead puppy on the table.

"Who killed it?" the newcomer persists.

"Nobody's sure," the coworker replies. "I think it was someone who left the organization a few months ago."

"Well that thing is kind of stiff and stinky," says the newcomer, feeling she needs to point out the obvious. "Why does Mary keep putting it on the table?"

"Like I said, it's very sensitive," whispers the coworker. "Mary brings it everywhere. You'll see her dragging it around with her wherever she goes. She puts it on the table at every meeting."

"Why doesn't Mary just bury the puppy?" the newcomer asks.

Everyone in the room is wondering the same thing—but nobody would dare ask Mary. They think she might bite.

Mary is not the only one who drags a dead puppy around the office. Lots of people can't let go of old grudges or can't accept that nobody else thinks their "pet" project is worth pursuing.

Maybe a company merger robbed you of your favorite part of the job. Or perhaps a coworker offended you once and you still give him the cold shoulder—even though you can't quite remember why you were so mad at him.

Those attitudes are "dead puppies."

Grace's dead puppy is the "old" way of doing things at her company.

She was the boss's assistant for more than twenty years before he retired. Now she's the new boss's assistant.

New Boss doesn't do things the way Old Boss did. Grace thinks he should.

So she drags that dead puppy like a sin she can't forgive all around the office with her.

Everybody knows she has it.

Everybody thinks she's ridiculous. It's in the way.

New Boss is getting ready to fire her.

Holding on to a dead puppy, after all, is the same as posting a big, bright—but empty—"Beware of Dog" sign on your house: People are afraid to approach.

They're afraid of your bite or your bark, so they stay away from you. They leave you out.

Grace's coworkers and Mary's are whispering behind their backs: "Get over it already! Bury the poor, dead thing! Have a funeral!"

That's what Grace did.

She surprised New Boss and everyone in the room when she announced at a staff meeting that she was going to bury her dead puppy.

She admitted that she resented New Boss for not continuing the business in the style of Old Boss, and she resented everyone else for going along with it.

She didn't want to lose her job, and she was ready to give up her grudge.

It was hard for her.

Not as hard as an actual funeral, of course, but hard enough.

In today's work environment, everyone must collaborate and work on teams.

We fool ourselves if we think teamwork can be effective while the Marys and Graces in the organization keep dragging their dead puppies around.

People who carry grudges, refuse to be cordial to others who offended them long ago, or can't get past an upsetting incident that everyone else has forgotten are tough to manage.

Pity the poor, new manager who unwittingly inherits a staff in need of a graveyard for all of their old hurts, missteps, and dead puppies.

If you recognize your own behavior in these stories of dead puppies, it's time to move on.

Which is more mature and responsible: to wholeheartedly do the job you're qualified and needed for and paid to do, or to wear a big sign that says "Beware of Dead Puppy"?

If you work with someone like Mary or Grace, do her a great favor.

Ignore her sign.

Push past your own fear of being bitten. Assume she wears the "Beware of Dog" sign as protection, but that it's an empty threat.

Reach out and include her in your next project.

Sure, she might bark at you.

More likely, though, she'll remove her sign and gratefully let you in, realizing that you just want to work together and pose no threat.

SELF-EMPOWERMENT STRATEGY #3: ME, ME, ME

My friend Janet was telling me about the boss she has to "put up with" as he continues to get promoted to his "level of incompetence."

"Why don't you look elsewhere?" I insisted. "Don't you know how incredible you are? Your talent far outstrips what you've been allowed to do for the organization. Where is your perspective?"

"Good point," she acknowledged. "I really haven't done anything to see what's out there and to understand, in an expanded sense, who I am."

Then she blurted out the all-time most common statement I hear from even remarkably talented people: "One day they'll notice how hard I have worked and realize I could do a much better job than my boss."

"Are you secretly hoping he'll just quit and you'll be the obvious choice to take his place?" I asked.

At first, she was incredulous. But eventually she admitted that's exactly what she was doing.

"I am waiting," she confided. "But I don't know why or for what."

Figuring that out will create for Janet a powerful awareness that is quite freeing.

Once she knows why she is waiting—instead of going after what she feels she deserves—she can begin to move forward.

Likewise, getting some perspective on why *you* are marching in place can be a powerful tool that will allow you to choose your future rather than wait for it to happen to you.

It's possible you will realize you are waiting for something that is unlikely to happen.

Once you do, you create a space for movement—*forward* movement.

Are you waiting to get noticed? Or are you secretly glad that nobody is noticing you?

Be honest.

When it comes down to it, if you kept a running catalog of your work-related accomplishments, you probably would be astonished at how much you have done.

Don't count on your boss or her boss to keep track of that for you.

They too often pay more attention to your screw-ups, bad-attitude days, and other negatives that can prevent your next move.

Be responsible for letting them know about the many good, important, and amazing feats you have accomplished during your time at the organization.

Before you can do that, you need to take stock of your accomplishments and triumphs.

Create a "self-empowerment" binder. Here's how:

Divide a loose-leaf binder into ten sections. Fill it with your back-patting, raise-deserving, promotion-worthy accomplishments!

Tab 1: Your résumé
Tab 2: A list of accomplishments that don't appear on the résumé
Tab 3: A tally of all your skills, talents, and abilities
Tab 4: Letters, thank-you notes, certificates of acknowledgment, and complimentary e-mails you have received

Tab 5:   Copies of peer-to-peer and manager-to-subordinate evaluations

Tab 6:   A list of your goals and your definition of success

Tab 7:   The self-examination tools you have used, like Myers-Briggs, Birkman, and the DISC behavioral assessment, for example

Tab 8:   Your dreams

Tab 9:   Your hobbies and community service activities

Tab 10 and beyond: Other categories of accomplishments that are uniquely yours

This exercise takes time, but it's worth it.

Don't resist the process because it is too "me" focused.

I know you already know all about yourself.

But others don't. Your bosses don't.

Putting it all in one place helps you realize how much you have going for you and what kinds of information you should be sharing with the higher-ups at work.

It's not your boss's responsibility to notice you and pluck you out of the crowded workforce for the promotion you know you deserve.

You are responsible for thinking of creative and innovative ways to let the organization know who you are.

If you don't, saying you are "overlooked" will be an understatement.

Face it: Managers and coworkers rarely know you beyond your "task" accomplishments. Those achievements are important, but it's not enough to simply accomplish tasks.

They need to know you can relate well to others, work efficiently as part of a team, think innovatively, adapt to new environments, value differences, and behave flexibly.

Put together that binder. Take a good look at a concrete compilation of who you are, what you have accomplished, and where you want to go.

Be responsible for your perspective. This is your "I" binder. Grow it.

Empower Your Time

If you think you have no control over how you spend your time, ask yourself this: Why are you allowing someone else to control something that belongs to you?

If you are overbooked and overburdened because you work overtime or go over and above what you know is comfortable and reasonable for you, you're the one who's out of control.

An employer, a coworker, a spouse, your friends, and even your kids can ask, demand, and cajole you to spend your time doing things you don't want to do, but they can't make you do them. They don't have the power.

You're the one with the power when it comes to your time and your schedule. You can say yes or you can say no.

But saying yes when you mean no—or even if you mean "Oh, no!"—is either a lie or an agreement to do something that you don't want to do or cannot possibly do well.

The three self-empowering strategies in this chapter show you that you are responsible for every time commitment you make.

SELF-EMPOWERMENT STRATEGY #4: SAY NO

No is an empowering word.

It's an honest word.

Finding the power to say *no* could be the very thing that makes you more successful.

Everybody knows somebody like my friend Lisa. Lisa just can't say *no.*

I suspect that she says *yes* so she'll be popular, or that she won't admit it when she doesn't want to do something, or that she doesn't think about all of her other commitments before she agrees to take on something else.

Whatever her reasoning, it landed her in jail.

I can't even picture Lisa in jail. She's a part-time kindergarten teacher's aide with two daughters of her own—smart, well-behaved 12-year-old twins. Even on weekends, her outfits match, her makeup is fresh, and her hair looks like she just came from the salon.

Everybody likes her. The neighborhood kids hang out at her house. Friends eagerly accept her frequent dinner invitations.

She volunteers at her church and at her kids' school. The annual neighborhood party is always in her yard. She cooks for the weekly team parties after her daughters' softball games, and she organizes ladies' night at the community pool once a month in the summer.

It was after ladies' night and four glasses of pinot grigio that she got arrested.

Everyone had such a good time, especially Lisa's sister-in-law, Pat, who drank a little too much wine. Realizing she was in no shape to drive home, she asked Lisa to give her a lift.

Lisa, who lives within walking distance of the pool where the ladies' night was held, had more wine than she would have if she had known she would be driving. She agreed anyway.

She paid for it when she made a right-hand turn on a one-way street—right into traffic going the other way.

She realized her mistake immediately and safely swerved onto the shoulder. But a police officer saw the whole thing.

When her husband came to pick the two women up from the police station, where Lisa had been fingerprinted and waited in handcuffs, he asked his wife why she agreed to drive after she had been drinking.

"Pat asked me to," was all she could come up with.

Pat isn't responsible for Lisa's decision. Pat isn't the one who agreed to drive after drinking four glasses of wine.

Lisa's *yes* was irresponsible.

Your *yes* might not have landed you in jail, but it has probably buried you under a pile of work, chores, favors, and commitments that you can't possibly honor—at least not in a thorough, thoughtful, complete way.

Saying *no* is very much a part of being personally responsible.

Agreeing to do things you don't want to do, don't have time to do, or know are wrong for you is irresponsible.

Being overwhelmed by the amount of work you have to do on the job, at home, or in your neighborhood is the #1 way you demonstrate irresponsibility.

Being overwhelmed jeopardizes your health, the clarity and quality of your thinking, and the quality of what you produce. It forces you to rush, to work when you're overtired, and to make mistakes.

Maybe you're getting something out of that.

Being overwhelmed is a convenient excuse for why you can't do something, why you can't finish something, or why your work is always full of mistakes.

It's a way to avoid being responsible for your actions.

I couldn't finish the project; there wasn't enough time. It's not my fault!

It makes you a victim—not of your work or your lack of time, but of yourself.

When I suggest to my clients that they say *no* to requests that will overwhelm them, they often reply, "I can't say no."

I can't say no.

You can't? Or you're *unwilling* to?

There's a huge difference.

The person who can't say *no* is a victim. The person who admits she is *unwilling* to say *no* is making a responsible statement.

She owns her decision to say *yes*. She knows what she's getting into: longer hours, less time for fun, sleepless nights, the repercussions of fatigue-induced mistakes.

Still, some people would rather say *yes* than to disappoint the boss or a spouse or a child. Some people would rather be overwhelmed and unhappy than to risk becoming unpopular.

If you are unwilling to say *no* at the expense of your health, free time and, in the extreme, your reputation for being a careful and credible worker, then by all means, say *yes!*

But *own* that decision.

Admit that it's your choice to say *yes* even though you feel overwhelmed because of it.

Don't blame it on your boss, your mother, your drunken sister-in-law, your kids, or circumstances beyond your control.

This is something you can control by uttering a single syllable: *No.*

The person who chooses to say *no* on the occasions when yes will wreak havoc on her life is acting responsibly.

She knows she might disappoint the person who is asking for the favor or trying to dump more work on her. She knows the job might get done differently—or perhaps not at all—without her input.

Still, she chooses not to agree to do something that she knows is going to overwhelm her, threaten her health, cost her sleep, or wind up full of errors and possibly even unfinished anyway.

If you're dead tired, overworked, and dragging through your day because you have so much to do, just say *no!*

Saying *yes* paints an unrealistic picture of what is possible in a person's day or how much can actually get done in the time available.

Empower yourself to say *no* on those occasions when yes is truly the wrong answer for you.

Still afraid nobody will like you if you do?

Try saying *no* in a very nice way.

I'm so flattered that you asked me! Thank you for asking! I'm humbled that you think I could manage an important job like that! But I have to say no. It sounds like a great project, and

I'm so glad you're the one in charge of it. I know you'll make it a success. I'm so sorry I won't be able to help you, but I won't. Good luck with it!

And review your personal definition of success.

Does it include an item that says, *Success to me is working until 8:00 P.M. every night, missing dinner with my family, and doing whatever anyone asks of me, even if it means I have no time to relax, take care of myself, or do the things I love?*

I'm sure it doesn't.

Think hard about your boss, your spouse, your children, your parents, and your friends.

Is any one of them going to "fire" you from their lives, disown you, cut you out of their will, or withdraw their love because you say you can't fit their project into your crowded schedule this week?

I'm sure they're not.

If someone says she will never speak to you again because you have declined to do a favor or take on a job, call her in a week and ask if she still loves you.

I'm sure she does.

If she doesn't, do you really want to stay in such a conditional relationship?

SELF-EMPOWERMENT STRATEGY #5: SCHEDULE CONSERVATIVELY

How do you know when no is a more responsible answer than yes?

Look at what else you have to do. Do you have enough time available to you to do all of that—well—and also successfully fill the request being made of you?

If so, go for it! If not, the answer has to be *no.*

If you keep a calendar that thoroughly details the demands on your time each day, the decision between *no* and *yes* will stare you right in the face.

Here's a strategy that works for me, and for hundreds of my clients who have changed the way they organize their days.

1. First, get rid of your to-do list.
   - It's good to keep a reminder of all the things you need to accomplish so you won't forget any of them. Still, writing them in a list form does not help you accomplish the tasks.
   - Keep track of your tasks on a calendar instead. Place each item on the date and at the time you intend to accomplish it.

2. Remove "to-do" items that you know you're never going to do.
   - Those are jobs that perpetually take up space on your long to-do list, but go untouched week after week. If you figure you'll hang onto them just in case you find some spare time one day—chances are, they're never going to get done.
   - Unburden yourself by letting them go.

3. Change your relationship with time.
   - Don't try to cram twelve hours of work into eight hours. Instead, write each task that you accept onto your calendar in a block of time. Estimate the amount of time it will take you to complete the task, and assign it the appropriate number of hours.

4. Estimate realistically.
   - If you've accepted the opportunity to give a speech, for example, block out enough time to do research, write, revise, practice, travel to the location of the speech, arrive early enough to deal with pre-performance jitters, deliver the speech, take questions, and travel back to the office.
   - That's a lot more time than it takes to simply write and deliver the speech. It's a more realistic amount of time—time you can block out on your calendar and plan to spend.
   - Likewise, if you have to attend a staff meeting, allot some time to prepare for the meeting as well as enough time to attend it.
   - This way, you can see at a glance whether you have time in your day to take on something new.
   - One glance will tell you whether your answer is *no* or *yes* when someone comes around asking for a favor or offloading a new assignment.
   - If you prepare a gigantic to-do list each morning, fully believing—or at least hoping—that there will be enough time to complete each item—you are holding yourself and others to unrealistic expectations.
   - Blocking out time for each task on your list shows you realistically what you will be able to accomplish in the amount of time available to you.
   - You'll be able to see just by looking at your calendar whether something new will fit into your day—or not.

5. Do not double book.
   - If you're going to accept a new, two-hour task, look at your calendar to see if two hours are available.
   - If you can't find them, tell your boss that you do not have the time it will require you to complete the task.
   - Ask or recommend which of your other two-hour assignments you can "trade" for the new one.
   - Do not simply accept the assignment without letting the boss know it will overwhelm you.

6. Empower yourself to show your boss what you can realistically accomplish in the time you have.

7. Leave some free time in each work day.
   - You need time to answer e-mails, return phone calls, handle emergencies, and regroup between the finish of one project and the start of a new one.

8. Complete each day completely.
   - During the course of the day, a phone call might have come in that left you with something unexpected to deal with, or perhaps you had a great idea that you want to pitch to the boss.
   - Choose not to interrupt your day to tend to those tangents unless they're urgent.
   - Instead, jot those tasks on a corner of your calendar as they come up.
   - At the end of the day, before you leave the office for the evening, find a place on your calendar the next day or

the next when you will have time to handle these things. Assign them a block of time.

- Choose not to let those small, unfinished jobs develop into a to-do list. You'll never get back to them if you do.

9. Acknowledge that you have limited time and energy.
   - You are human. If you only have eight cylinders, you can't run on nine; it's just not possible.
   - Racing to complete an unrealistic to-do list is a choice that inevitably will burn you out, and then you'll be no good to your boss, your team, your company, your family, your friends, or yourself.
   - It's not really so heroic to work twelve hours a day so you can accomplish everything everybody wants you to. Those kinds of heroes eventually become unproductive.
   - Instead, resolve to be fully present in your day—in each task—and to complete each day completely.
   - Allow yourself the time to do that, and empower yourself to say *no* when the demands exceed what you consider to be realistic.
   - If the boss says, "Of course you can squeeze this extra project into your schedule," tell her, "I cannot do that, given everything else that is on my schedule. Which of my other projects can we drop in order to take this on?"
   - Be firm, be clear.
   - Say *no!*

Certainly, there are times when we all need to put in an extra-ordinary effort, to work overtime, to finish something that takes longer than we expected or longer than the work day.

Rise to those occasions, but *do not let them become routine.* You make them routine by overbooking yourself when you say yes to becoming overwhelmed even when it's not a critical time.

People might say you're not a team player if you say *no;* that if you're not killing yourself (literally) over the job, you're not working for the good of the whole.

Those people made that up. It's not true, but it's a popular strategy as organizations ask employees to work harder so they get by with fewer workers.

It's to no one's benefit for you to be overwhelmed, unhappy, or exhausted.

But if that's your definition of success, go for it!

SELF-EMPOWERMENT STRATEGY #6: MAKE AN APPOINTMENT

Some people are just too hard to say *no* to.

They are demanding bosses, needy children, people who anger easily, people whom you love.

Are you choosing to say *yes* to someone—even when you would prefer to say *no*—because you want to avoid feeling that person's wrath or causing her disappointment?

Empower yourself to change the way you react when that person makes an unreasonable demand of you.

Talk to that person about the problem.

Schedule a time for that conversation.

Don't try to talk about it during the heat of a confrontation, when you or the other person is angry or overwhelmed. Make an appointment to talk about it with your manager, your spouse, your mother—whoever it is.

The purpose of the conversation is for you to learn how to say no to that person. If it's your boss, the conversation might go something like this:

> The reason I'm talking to you right now is because I'm having trouble saying *no* to the extra work that has been coming my way. My concern is that I'm getting so buried that I'm not going to be able to complete all of this work in a quality way.
>
> I've also noticed that when I get an assignment that I know I can't manage because I already have a full schedule with as many deadlines as I can handle, I'm afraid to say *no*.
>
> I need some help figuring out what to do.
>
> Is it that I'm not prioritizing the tasks correctly? Is it because I don't work fast enough?
>
> I'm afraid this problem is going to get bigger, so I'm here to try to clarify what's expected of me.
>
> Can you give me your input?

Right about then, you might start wishing you had just said *yes* and missed your own birthday party so you could finish the work.

Confronting someone you find hard to refuse is scary.

When you do it, you rock the boat. You invite a reaction that you can neither predict nor control from the boss or whomever you're confronting.

In the moment, you've chosen truth over peace.

Yes, it's scary stuff. But it's brave. It's self-empowering, like Lea's leap into the pool. And it's a means toward a worthwhile end.

On the bright side, not too many managers would explode with anger or toss someone out of the office when an employee comes to them with such an honest appeal.

The manager might be surprised, even caught off guard, by the employee's courage and honesty.

Few people think of themselves as too demanding or unapproachable, and most will respond positively (albeit a bit shyly) to the suggestion that their behavior is making another person feel smaller or ineffective.

I say that with confidence because I can be one of those scary people, only I didn't know it!

Empower Your Words

What you choose to say to others and about others has an impact on your success and your reputation.

Likewise, the way you respond to what others say to you can determine whether you successfully influence a situation, help a friend or coworker, or turn people away.

The word *you* for example, can sound accusatory. The word *but* can dash the hopes of the person you're speaking to—even if you have something positive to say afterward.

What you say and how you say it is up to you. The four self-empowering strategies in this chapter will help you evaluate whether you're choosing words that impede your success or help make it happen.

SELF-EMPOWERMENT STRATEGY #7: I'M OKAY; ARE YOU OKAY?

One of my employees at a previous company confronted me much in the way I'm suggesting you confront your boss or another person in your life to whom you have a hard time saying *no*.

I am a focused, no-nonsense person when it comes to getting my work done. I decided a long time ago to be present in the moment, no matter what I was doing. That works for me.

I concentrate on my work while I'm at work, so I'm able to complete each day fully and leave the office with a clear head. I bring that clear head home to my husband and children, and I am able to be completely present with them while I'm at home.

It's great.

For me.

My staff apparently didn't think my work habits were so great.

Three days after a staff meeting with the nine employees who reported to me, one of them crept into my office, slinked around to the side of the big desk that I used to keep distance between myself and everyone else, and gently asked, "Are you okay?"

I was, indeed, "okay."

In fact, I was on a roll.

I'd had a brilliant idea in the car on my commute to work and had torn into the office, made a beeline for my computer, and started pounding on it.

I hadn't even stopped to say "Hello" to my staff.

"Yes, David, I'm okay. Why do you ask?"

And then I remembered: "Are you okay?" is a code.

It really means, *"Why didn't you say 'Hello' to anyone when you got here this morning? Are you mad? Are you sick? Did the staff do something wrong?"*

During the staff meeting three days earlier, after reading my staff-generated performance evaluations—for the umpteenth time—saying that my employees think I'm "moody," I had confronted them.

Frankly, I didn't understand the comment. I produced results at work. My team always met the deadlines, usually under budget. I demonstrated tremendous business acumen and a knack for navigating the office politics that cause most people to run and hide.

What did they mean by calling me "moody"? I demanded.

As my employees stared at their shoes, it dawned on me that demanding feedback might not be the best way to get it. So I issued an appeal.

"I honestly don't know what you mean when you say I'm moody," I admitted. "I need examples."

Only David was willing to speak.

"Some days you come in and all is right with the world. Other times we don't know if we did something wrong or if you have an upset stomach or what, but you don't give us so much as a 'Hello' and you look unhappy.

"Or mean. Or, um, something."

They want me to say "Hello" and smile? What's that about?

I was incredulous. I wanted to blurt out, "You have got to be kidding me," but I didn't.

That uncharacteristic act of restraint made me feel uncomfortably proud. So I asked, "What else?"

Two or three other employees sheepishly gave examples of my being short with people or seeming unreceptive. Still, I didn't "get" it.

So I invited some "real-time" information.

"When I am doing this behavior in the future, it would be great if you would clue me in," I volunteered. "When you see it, ask me—as it's happening—'Are you okay?' That will be a code that means I need to pay attention to my behavior."

The next thing I knew, David was walking into my office and asking if I'm okay.

It was a real eye-opener.

It seems several employees were in the office when I arrived that morning. I walked right past them without so much as a "Hello," slammed a file on my desk, and excitedly began pounding away at my keyboard. It threw them all off.

David might as well have hit me on the head with a 2-by-4.

At that moment, he helped me see my behavior through my staff's eyes. He taught me that as their leader, my behavior and even my mood affects them greatly, even when I don't say anything.

Or maybe especially when I don't.

From my perspective, I was justified in rushing past them so I could record every detail of my great idea before I forgot it.

To me, I was focused, not moody. I'm focused *a lot*.

Apparently, their perception of me was different.

Until I was willing to really understand what an enormous impact my behavior had on my staff, I wasn't likely to change it.

During our next staff meeting, I thanked David for having the courage to confront me by using the code we had agreed upon.

It is courageous, after all, to approach a moody boss!

It turned out that David—who was squirming as I praised him in front of his colleagues—had been nudged through my office door that morning.

"It really wasn't courage," he admitted. "They paid me ten bucks to go in and talk to you."

Everyone laughed—including me. I left the meeting in a great mood.

SELF-EMPOWERMENT STRATEGY #8: HAVE A "YOU-ECTOMY"

Got a problem with someone?

Leave him out of the conversation.

Charlotte wants her husband, Matt, to pitch in more often with the housework. Which approach do you think will be more effective?

Approach #1: You never do anything around here. All you do is sit around and watch TV. You're the one who made the mess. You're the one who should clean it up!

Approach #2: I'm so worn out from my week that I don't think I can clean the whole house by myself this weekend. I could really use some help.

Aside from being less hysterical in Approach #2, Charlotte uses the word *I* instead of *you* to make her point.

You is a word that's wrought with accusation.

For the best chance for a successful conversation, don't use it unless you're asking the person for feedback ("What do you think?").

Instead, use the words *I, me*, and *my*.

To the listener, your appeal will sound like you are taking responsibility for the situation rather than blaming him for it.

Use phrases like:

- I'm frustrated because I can't get all of this work done . . .
- I don't understand the way I'm being talked to . . .
- I need help understanding this . . .
- I need more resources and feedback.

Have a you-ectomy.

The accusatory "you" is out. The responsible "I" is in.

That's different from the selfish "me."

Get the word *you* out of your vocabulary as much as possible.

An approach with your husband might go like this:

> I'm confused. I understood the agreement to be that the garbage would be out on the curb on Tuesday. Today is Wednesday, but the garbage is still in the kitchen. Did I misunderstand the agreement? Was I mistaken about which day the garbage needs to go out?

His answer, of course, will be, "No, you didn't misunderstand."

He won't be happy, but he won't be able to say you have accused him of anything, either, because you haven't.

You've talked only about your own understanding, not about his misdeed.

In your part of the conversation, you reveal how you feel, what you understood about the situation or the agreement, and what you hope to gain from this talk (clarification, feedback, more resources, or a new agreement, for instance).

I reserve *you* for conversations in which I am giving a direct warning to someone, and I want no ambiguity about what I am saying.

Even then, I use it sparingly.

When you rarely utter the word *you*, it's quite effective when you do use it:

> The agreement was that work started every day at 8:00 A.M. It is now 8:45, and this is the third time this has happened. I will issue a written reprimand today. You need to be clear about this: You are in a probationary period. You will be fired if you come to work late again.

SELF-EMPOWERMENT STRATEGY #9: THE MAGIC OF "AND"

Mark and Amber had just sunk their life savings into a condominium at the beach, and they wanted to recoup part of their expenses by renting it out during the summer.

On the advice of their realtor, Amber called Roberta, who is in charge of the realty office's rental program.

"We can do it for you," Roberta told Amber, "but you're not going to make as much money as you would if you handled the rentals yourself."

Amber, who works full-time, didn't want to handle the rentals herself, she explained to Roberta. She wanted the realty office to do it.

"We'll handle it, but we're going to charge you 20 percent of the revenue," Roberta continued.

"Do you have a Website that will show our condo?" asked Amber.

"Yes, but the photos are pretty small."

"Could you come over to see the place?"

"I need to see it, but I don't have time this week. I'll come over, but not until next Monday."

Amber asked Roberta why she was so negative.

"I'm not negative," Roberta responded. "I just want to present you with the worst-case scenario so you won't expect too much."

Amber said, "Good-bye" and called a different realty office.

"Can you rent our condo for us?" she asked.

"We can do it for you, and you stand to make at least half of what you would take in if you rented it yourself—without doing any of the work," came the reply.

"Do you charge a fee for your service?"

"We'll handle everything for you and we only charge 20 percent."

"Do you have a Website?"

"We show photos of every condo we rent, and people love them. They're small and they give people an at-a-glance tour of the accommodations and the view."

"Can you come over and see the place?"

"I need to see it, and I can be there at noon on Monday."

Amber hired Realty Company #2.

The difference between a negative conversation and a positive one rested on a single word: *and*.

Learn to use the word *and* to move things along. It is a great substitute for *but*.

But ends the listener's hope. *And* moves the conversation forward.

I heard a saying once: "Follow your 'but' and you will know where you are."

Some examples:

- I appreciate your idea, but that isn't feasible given what I've been hearing about the budget.
- I'd give you what you want, but I inherited a team that doesn't know how to work together.
- I know you need a vacation, but we can't afford a trip to the beach.

If reading these statements doesn't make the hair on the back of your neck stand up, what's wrong with you?

They make me absolutely crazy.

Change one word, and change the entire situation:

- I appreciate your idea *and* I will make it a priority as soon as the budget becomes available. I'll keep you informed every two weeks as to status.
- I will give you what you want *and*, because I'm part of a team I am not totally familiar with, I'll get back to you in one week about how fast I can deliver. I need to understand my team before I overcommit.
- I know you need a vacation, *and* I'll make a trip to the beach a priority as soon as we pay off our credit card debt.

At every opportunity, change *but* to *and*, and feel the power.

When I use this method to interact with others, it moves things forward, especially among those taking the victim stance.

I understand the computer won't let you do what you want, and *let's take the next step to resolve the problem.*

I see that the report isn't complete, and *here is what I expect you to do to meet the deadline.*

No matter what, no matter where, if I can change a statement that blames someone else or portrays someone as a victim of circumstances, I will do it.

I will validate the person's feelings, and then add the word *and.*

It takes practice, and if the primary focus is on results and competence, it gets easier.

Would you like to stop following everyone else's "but"? Start by making sure no one is following yours.

SELF-EMPOWERMENT STRATEGY #10: GET OFF THE GOSSIP-GO-ROUND

Craig is a young pharmacist who hated his job.

Just as he was getting the hang of the routine at work, a new boss changed the routine.

She told the staff she had two goals: to offer better customer service and to transform the pharmacy into a great place to work.

"Both goals are about people," she said. "People are our reason for being in business. And the people who work here are our greatest asset."

Craig's knee-jerk reaction: "That's a bunch of bull," he told his fellow pharmacists. "If we're so important, then why doesn't she let us do things our way instead of changing everything around?"

Craig viciously put the boss and her new ways down— behind her back, of course—and resisted learning her new routine.

His coworkers were more than willing to join in. They started rumors, told lies, belittled, and even cursed the new boss.

Craig thought this kind of talk would help him get his resentment out of his system.

It did the opposite. It made him miserable.

It's no surprise that his boss didn't appreciate Craig's surly attitude.

She kept him at arm's length, exchanging only cool pleasantries.

She stopped asking for his input and refused his requests for a different schedule and more challenging assignments.

At the same time, Craig's gossipy coworkers started to seem vindictive and mean.

Again, no surprise. Their words and behavior *were* vindictive and mean.

So were Craig's.

He started to dread the start of the work day.

As he sulked over his bad luck and a batch of antibiotics one afternoon, his thoughts wandered back to pharmacy school, where he had taken a seminar in personal responsibility and mutual respect.

Gossip, he had learned, hurt the one doing the bad-mouthing as much as it hurt his target.

At the time, he told classmates the tenet was "bull."

Now he wasn't so sure.

It started to sink in that his own behavior was causing his unhappiness at work.

Once he became responsible for his doldrums, he realized the boss and her new routine weren't causing his problems. *He* was.

So he hopped off the Gossip-Go-Round and empowered himself to take a risk that would allow him to get what he wanted: more challenging work, a better schedule, and a day that began without dread.

He decided to approach his boss with his questions about her new routine. He decided to put aside his bad attitude, his demands, and his accusations, at least for the sake of the conversation he was about to have.

The boss sensed the change in him. She explained her routine and asked Craig to give it a chance.

He did.

He found that her routine really did improve the way the pharmacy ran and gave the pharmacists more time to spend conferring with customers.

Craig empowered himself to be responsible for his success and comfort level at work.

He empowered himself to stop gossiping.

He resolved to change his situation by making better choices.

Whether you work one on one with a coworker or as part of a larger team, your day will go smoother for yourself and for them, too, once you eliminate gossip from your routine.

Completely.

Instead of talking *about* your colleagues, talk *to* them.

If you are 100 percent responsible for working well with your coworkers, you absolutely cannot gossip about them. If you do, know the result you're creating. And own it.

Gossip is difficult to pull away from because it seems so interesting. It's like rubber-necking at the scene of an accident. We want to look.

It makes us feel included.

Still, the only intent of gossip is to undermine the reputation of someone else.

Think about it: When you hear gossip about someone, doesn't your perception of that person take a negative turn? *I'm not surprised Katie won the sales award this month. She's been awfully chummy with the boss lately, if you know what I mean!*

Communication that enhances another person is not gossip. *That Katie works hard and knows her stuff. She really deserves the sales award!*

Repeating facts and information is not gossip. *Katie sold twice as much this month as she did last month. Wow!*

In the work environment, gossip can undermine a colleague, demoralize the ones who are being talked about, and totally trash any efforts at team building, trust, and honest communication.

By participating in gossip, you are making a statement—through your words and actions—that you have no interest in creating a trusting, honest environment.

The way to stop office gossip—which has no redeeming value—is to stop your own participation in it.

It's an individual decision, but it's not always easy.

It wasn't easy for Craig.

His pharmacist "friends" turned around and started gossiping about him once he declined to participate in their water-cooler secret-sharing.

They said he wasn't a team player.

They called him a snob.

They said he had a "thing" for the new boss.

I say, *So what?*

They can say it 100 times. That won't make it true.

Get off the Gossip-Go-Round. Here's how:

- Inform your gossip buddies that you are no longer interested in talking about people behind their backs.
- When someone brings gossip to you, tell her you would like to share her negative information with the person she's talking about. Even better, invite her to tell the person herself.
- Let your coworkers know that you are committed to talking directly with anyone you are having a problem with. Suggest that they do the same.
- Ask your colleagues to hold you accountable to your commitment. Ask them to remind you of your pledge if they hear you gossiping. They'll be *glad* to rub your face in it.

These are risky moves.

It's always risky to empower yourself to be and do better.

In no time, you'll be dropped from the gossip ring.

Can you handle these so-called friends cutting you loose because you won't gossip with them any more?

You know they're going to gossip about *you*.

They probably have been all along. Weren't you gossiping about them, too, when they had their backs turned?

Embrace your freedom. The eventual result is quite positive.

You'll be perceived as someone who can be trusted not to talk behind someone else's back.

Your integrity level and reputation will improve.

That will benefit you far more than gossip.

Getting off of the Gossip-Go-Round takes discipline. You might not be able to go cold turkey.

Once you rid yourself of that nasty habit, though, the benefits can be tremendous.

Think of how much time you'll save if you don't spend your time engaging in bad-mouthing your grudge-holding "friends" in the coffee room.

It's also a personal development exercise that can leave you with a sense of wholeness and integrity.

The Accountability
Quotient, Part 2

S elf-empowerment is taking the actions—and the risks—
that you need to in order to ensure that you achieve the
results you desire.

Are you more authoritarian (command and control) or
team oriented (build the ability of individuals to work inter-
dependently together)? Are you more comfortable in a hier-
archical or flat organization? Do you hold others to live up to
what they are capable of and support their self-empowerment?
Or do you rush in to rescue, fix, and save everyone else at the
expense of yourself—just so you'll be liked?

This chapter will help you measure your level of self-
empowerment. On *Exhibit 4*, use a scale from zero to 5 (zero is
"none" and 5 is "100 percent") to rate your own willingness to
take the risks and actions you need to get what you want. (The
guidelines following the grid will help you interpret your result.)

EXHIBIT 4. Your Self-Empowerment Quotient

Category	Best Possible	Accumulated Score
Empowerment		50
Questions	*Rating Distribution*	

1. I am accountable for whatever happens in my organization, regardless of how well I do my job.

    0   1   2   3   4   5

2. I trust that most of my coworkers will perform well if given greater authority over their own jobs.

    0   1   2   3   4   5

3. I give coworkers timely feedback regarding their job performance.

    0   1   2   3   4   5

4. I believe all human beings are capable of outstanding performance, irrespective of differences.

    0   1   2   3   4   5

5. For the most part, I am nonjudgmental and accept people as they are.

    0   1   2   3   4   5

EXHIBIT 4. *(Continued)*

Category	Best Possible	Accumulated Score
Empowerment		50
Questions		*Rating Distribution*

6.	Relationships work best when you hold people to their commitments.	0	1	2	3	4	5
7.	I hold others accountable for achieving mutually agreed-upon performance goals.	0	1	2	3	4	5
8.	I can depend on coworkers to responsibly perform work assignments.	0	1	2	3	4	5
9.	I find it easy to trust my coworkers.	0	1	2	3	4	5
10.	I believe overall that my coworkers are committed to my professional success.	0	1	2	3	4	5

INTERPRET YOUR SCORE

High

If your responses add up to between 40 and 50, you are achieving the 85% Solution! Your score (80%–100%) indicates that you will thrive in an environment of self-empowerment. You likely know when a group working together needs to be a self-managed team or when a well-managed environment will be more effective for getting to the agreed-upon result. You will find it easy to provide examples of how you empower yourself, and you are willing to ask for the authority you need to take the actions and risks necessary to achieve results.

Medium

A score of between 30 and 40 indicates that you have a need, at times, to be managed. Falling between 60% and 70% reveals that you may want others to notice your hard work and reward you. You are less likely to take the initiative to be clear about exactly what is expected of you or to make clear agreements up front. If interpersonal challenges need to be resolved in your immediate work environment or on your team, you will likely wait for a manager or someone else to address them. It is time to take a hard look at and improve your interpersonal skills.

Low

If your score totals less than 30, you will tend to do best in a closely managed, structured, rule-based environment. A score of 0% to 50% indicates that if others are the source of dissatisfaction in your work or life, it will be important to stay off the Gossip-Go-Round. Instead, find someone who can do something about your problems, and take your problems to that person. You tend to be very low risk in relationships and choose peace over truth. If you are the smartest in a group, you may tend to finger-point and blame when things go wrong, expect others to step up around you, and see no solution that you can be a part of until others come up to your speed or see it your way. Some may see you as wanting to be right over being effective.

PART III

Personal Accountability

It Goes Both Ways

Debbie was three months away from becoming the first person in her family to graduate from college, and she looked forward to an easy final semester.

For her senior project, she was assigned to work on a three-member team to create a marketing plan for a fictitious company. Her professor estimated that it would take each member of the team at least four full-time weeks to complete the work, and the project was worth 50 percent of each student's grade.

Debbie met with her group the first week of school, eager to dispense with the semester's lone academic challenge. Her close friend, Emma, was a teammate. So was Meredith, a classmate Debbie didn't know very well.

At the meeting, Meredith told Debbie and Emma that her sister had done the same paper for her senior project at another university and had earned an A on it.

The three of them could submit the sister's project as their own, Meredith proposed. Nobody would ever know because it came from a different school.

Debbie was reluctant and said so. She had never cheated on a school project before. Emma, on the other hand, loved the idea of getting out of the work.

She and Meredith pressured Debbie into going along with the plan, and Debbie eventually agreed.

After a while, Debbie started to look forward to the A she would receive without doing any work. She and Emma laughed about it and asked each other if they wanted to "go to the library to work on the project" when they were really headed for the mall.

They didn't laugh when all three failed the course after the professor, during a routine plagiarism check, discovered that the students had submitted somebody else's paper.

Debbie blamed Meredith and Emma.

She told the professor it was their idea.

She insisted she was opposed to the plan and that they had pressured her into going along with it.

No luck.

Debbie was not allowed to graduate. She had to repeat the course.

Instead of basking in her success and bragging about her easy A as she planned, Debbie was denying that she was accountable for her failure.

But she is.

Saying you're not accountable doesn't mean you're not accountable.

Debbie was responsible for getting a good grade on the project during the first meeting with Meredith and Emma.

She empowered herself to take the risk—cheating—that would get her what she wanted: an easy A and graduation.

Now that she has her F, she can't change what she did.

She can't change how accountable she is.

She's every bit as accountable for her failure as she would have been for her success.

Whether she wants to be or not.

Her teacher is holding her accountable. The school is holding her accountable. Her parents are holding her accountable.

Whether she admits it or not, she is accountable for her own choices and actions.

We all are accountable for our own choices and actions.

Every time we choose something, we are accountable for that choice.

If Debbie had this mind-set, she either would have made a different choice—she wouldn't have cheated—or she would have admitted that she did and accepted the consequences without blaming others for her own bad judgment.

Denying that you're accountable doesn't make you any less accountable.

And you know it.

Accountability is a personal willingness—after the fact—to answer for the outcomes produced by your choices and actions.

If your actions result in a win, you're accountable for them.

If your choices land you in a heap of trouble, you're accountable for them.

Accountability is the third and final critical step necessary for any successful project or relationship:

Be accountable for your actions. Show that you are willing to answer for the outcomes that result from your choices, behaviors, and actions.

The first two steps are personal responsibility, which I discussed in Part I, and self-empowerment, which I covered in Part II.

Unlike responsibility, which is your mind-set before the fact, and empowerment, which is what enables the act itself, personal accountability happens after all is said and done.

While it's no small feat to stand up and say, "I am responsible for this choice even if it produces a bad outcome," that's still a lot easier than standing up after everyone knows the outcome is bad, and saying "I still own this, even though it's a disaster. You can hold me accountable. It was my choice. I'm responsible."

Just as a responsible person chants the mantra, before the fact, "no fault, no blame, no guilt," so does the accountable person, even after the outcome is known.

The accountable person doesn't get to change her mind about who is responsible once she learns that she has created a mess.

Stand Up

My husband says my job is to make grown men cry.

Chief executive officers. Human resource executives. Hospital administrators. Company presidents. *Him.*

They weep like babies.

My job *isn't* to make them cry, of course; it's simply to hold them accountable. It's being held accountable that makes them cry.

Being held accountable upsets most people. *Being* accountable upsets most people. Does it upset you?

If someone is telling you that you need to be accountable for something, it's probably because you've already messed up by not doing what you were supposed to do or what you promised you would do.

That's embarrassing, and uncomfortable, and upsetting.

Dry your eyes. Crying isn't going to get it done.

Instead of blubbering about all of the excuses why you didn't hold up your end of the deal, hold *yourself* accountable.

Personally accountable.

Save yourself some time: Stop making excuses. Nobody believes them anyway.

Not even you.

Then hold up your end. Do the work. Honor the commitment you made. Get on with it.

Of course if everyone did that, I'd be out of a job, and *I'd* be the one crying!

Back to my point.

People who are accountable for the outcomes of their choices and actions are happier than those who aren't—even when it means they have to grit their teeth, swallow their pride, and be responsible for their occasional failures.

You will be happier if you are personally accountable. I guarantee it.

Accepting the consequences of an unpopular action or a mistake is hard for anyone to do, but if you do it consistently, you will feel good about yourself, and the people around you will feel good about you, too.

That seems hard to believe when you're taking the heat for an embarrassing blunder, but it's true.

The people you deal with will trust you, count on you, and respect you.

Best of all, they will know what to expect from you.

So stand up and own what's yours, even if things didn't turn out as you planned.

Stand up and be accountable for your deeds—and your misdeeds, no matter how unintentional—instead of blaming your failures on other people or outside conditions.

Stand up even when you know you can get away with hiding your role in a calamity or with blaming it on someone else.

Be a stand-up person. Be personally accountable for your choices and actions.

What You'll Give Up

Y ou have much to gain by becoming a responsible,
self-empowered, accountable person: greater control over
your actions and over your success.

You also have a lot to lose.

J. T. lost sleep.

He's in charge of a 50-employee department at a midsized
organization that sells training and publications to small
businesses.

The company is strict about enforcing an 8:30 A.M. to
5:30 P.M. schedule for all employees, as it's important for
small business owners to be able to reach anyone they need
during business hours.

Top managers like J. T. allow themselves a bit of leeway
with those hours, feeling they have earned the privilege to
sleep a few minutes later in the morning over a long career

and a long tenure with this firm. J. T. routinely arrives between 9:00 and 9:30 A.M. but expects his staff to be there on time.

One editor was chronically late. She, too, strolled in between 9:00 and 9:30 every morning. She also worked until 6:00 or 6:30 every evening.

J. T. asked her to arrive earlier.

She didn't.

He chastised her. No luck.

Denied her an otherwise-deserved raise. Still late.

Put her on probation. Nope.

He didn't want to fire her. She was his best editor. So finally, he sat her down and asked her why she was late.

"I'm just not a morning person," she explained. "Like you, I feel better and work better if I can get started a little later in the morning."

Like you.

J. T.'s own reaction startled him. He started sweating.

"I'm usually here by the time you are," the editor continued, "and I work later. I always get my work done on time, even if I'm not here on time. Why is this a problem?"

Now J. T.'s throat was dry. How was he supposed to say, "Everyone has to follow the rules," when he wasn't following them?

How was he supposed to hold this woman accountable when he wasn't holding himself to the same standard?

The next day, J. T. set his alarm for 5:00 A.M. so he could get to work by 8:30. He was *mad.*

Mad at the editor? Not really, but that's how he treated her—like it was her fault he had to get up before the sun for his two-hour commute.

The editor was right: He's not a morning person.

Worse, he wasn't being responsible for his behavior. He was saying one thing—"Everybody has to be here on time"—and doing another—showing up an hour late every day.

His excuse and the editor's excuse were the same. Why was it okay for him and not for her?

The first time he set his alarm for the crack of dawn, he knew it wasn't okay, and that it had never been.

That epiphany stunned him.

And yes, it made him angry. He didn't *want* to be held accountable for his irresponsible actions. He's the boss.

He didn't *want* to forfeit his comfortable routine and what he considered his executive privilege.

But he's the boss.

J. T. is not the first high-ranking, successful executive I've met who believed he was accountable and was stunned to learn he wasn't.

He's not the first big shot whose mind-set changed when he realized he had to answer for his actions, even when they produced a poor result. He had to own his choices.

I meet bosses like J. T. all the time who ask me to bring my message of personal responsibility and personal accountability to their employees.

As if they don't need to hear it themselves.

When they do, it knocks them over to learn how often they try to deflect blame and fault so they don't have to answer for their own choices.

Personal accountability is something that *every* person needs, not just the ones you want to hold accountable. They will hold *you* accountable, too.

That's because you can't mandate accountability. You can only demonstrate it.

What are you doing that you're not allowing your employees, your children, or your friends to do? You might have to give that up.

Committing accountability is hard work.

When you choose accountability, you close that huge gap between what you say you are responsible for and what you do.

When you choose accountability, you become perfectly clear about what you expect of others. When you are not clear, you admit that it's not reasonable to hold others to your expectations or undeclared standards.

When you choose accountability, you stop finding scapegoats who can take the fall for you if one of your decisions causes a problem.

When you choose accountability, you don't get mad at someone else for calling you on it when you lapse. You welcome the reminder.

Choosing accountability takes courage.

Choosing accountability takes change.

Some of those changes might be uncomfortable. Some might be time consuming. Some might create extra work for you.

You might have to wake up earlier in the morning, start meeting every deadline, honoring every agreement you make.

Do you want to?

It's okay to say *no*. It's okay to choose not to be accountable.

It's powerful to say *yes*, to do the hard work and to reap the benefits of the transformation that will occur in you.

J. T. said *yes* and he chose accountability, but his story didn't end as you might think.

The 5:00 A.M. wake-up call just wasn't for him. So he did the accountable thing: He chose to take an early retirement.

The editor? She quit shortly afterward and now works for a company that offers flextime.

Tell the Truth

How would things have played out differently for President Bill Clinton if he had never uttered that famous denial about intern Monica Lewinsky: "I did not have sexual relations with that woman"?

The statement, of course, turned out to be a lie, and the president was impeached, in part, because that lie made it clear that he had told another lie to a grand jury.

Today, the dark cloud of dishonesty sullies his legacy as president.

What if he had admitted the truth?

"Yes, I had an inappropriate relationship with a young woman who is not my wife. I regret it. I can't excuse it. I am responsible for it."

He would have been branded a playboy and an adulterer (the same labels he wears anyway, even though he told the lie), but perhaps he would not have been accused of lying to a grand jury, which eventually led to his impeachment.

How about I. Lewis "Scooter" Libby, convicted of lying to a grand jury and the FBI about who told him the identity of CIA agent Valerie Plame, which he later revealed to journalists?

Prosecutors say he lied to protect his bosses, who are said to have been the ones who told him about Plame, and to salvage his own government career, which ended with his indictment.

If he had told the truth, his bosses would have been outed and his career would have been over. Same result.

The upside of the truth—and it's a big one: He wouldn't have been convicted of perjury or of obstructing justice.

Lying didn't help him at all. His White House job is over anyway. On top of that, he will forever be known as a liar.

See where I'm going with this?

Everybody screws up sometimes. Lying about it, blaming it on someone else, or hiding your involvement pretty much always makes it worse.

Do you live life on Planet I *Wish* I Hadn't Done That So I'll Say I Didn't? Do you figure if enough people believe your lie, it will magically become the truth?

Come *on!*

Get on Planet What *Is*.

You did what you did. You didn't do what you didn't do. Denying it won't change it. Blaming someone else for "making" you do it, or leaving you no choice, or forcing your hand, won't change it.

It's done. It's just What *Is*.

Surely you had a reason for doing what you chose to do. Own your reason.

Even if it's a reason other people regard as slimy—even if it's a reason *you* regard as slimy—it's your reason.

Stand up for your reason.

Apologize if your reasoning led to a mistake or a bad deed. Defend your reasoning if you believe you did the right thing. Be accountable.

Valerie Plame has accused Mr. Libby and others in the administration for ruining her career—and potentially putting her in danger—by revealing her secret identity as a CIA agent. She has alleged that they did it to retaliate against her husband, Ambassador Joseph Wilson, for writing that President George W. Bush lied about the intelligence he received before starting the war in Iraq.

Suppose that's all true.

What if Mr. Libby had told the country that he leaked her identity because he believed Mr. Wilson's writing was damaging to the country, to the U.S. troops in Iraq, and to the president's reputation? What if he said he agreed with those in the administration who said Wilson should be punished for what they considered to be a betrayal of the president?

Suppose he said, "Yes, I did it. I chose to do it. Here's why."

Many people would have disagreed with his motives and his actions, but some would have agreed.

He might still have gotten into legal trouble for revealing Ms. Plame's identity. But consider the consequence of his lying about it compared with the consequence of his telling the truth.

Because he lied:

1. He was convicted of perjury, obstruction of justice, and making false statements to a grand jury and the FBI.

He was not convicted for revealing Ms. Plame's identity to
the media. (President Bush commuted Mr. Libby's
30-month sentence so he didn't have to go to jail.)
2. He resigned from his coveted job in the Bush
administration.
3. He was sued in civil court by Mr. Wilson and Ms. Plame.
(A judge dismissed the suit.)
4. A *New York Times* reporter spent 85 days in jail.

If Mr. Libby had held himself accountable for his choice
to reveal Ms. Plame's identity, he could have saved himself
and the country and that reporter a lot of time and trouble
for the same outcome, minus the scourge of being branded
a liar.

Coming clean might not save you from the consequences
of your mistakes or your willfully bad actions. But saying,
"I did it. I'm accountable. Nobody else is to blame" at least
shows you have the integrity to answer for your crimes.

And it saves you the trouble of keeping track of your lies,
making enemies out of those you blame, and carving out a
reputation as a person who lacks integrity.

We can apply this mind-set to all kinds of high-profile liars
whose deceit wound up costing them more than the crime
they were trying to cover up: Martha Stewart, who spent time
in jail after saying she couldn't remember if an insider had
tipped her off before she sold some bad stock. Gary Hart, who
lied about his adultery and quashed his presidential aspira-
tions. The liars at Enron.

Americans are starving for accountability. We want those
at the root cause of our economic dilemmas to be accountable.
Greed can't be the bottom line; that's too simple.

Tell us your reasoning. Defend it. Be accountable.

Back to the rest of us.

Apply that mind-set to the workplace.

Example: A nurse who mistakenly gives a patient the wrong medicine but denies her error could compound the misstep by hiding the truth.

She doesn't want to get in trouble, but if she doesn't reveal what happened, her patient could be less likely to get an antidote that could save his life.

Even if the nurse is never fingered for her error, she will spend an inordinate amount of time and worry hiding it, lying to coworkers and even friends about what happened, keeping her story straight, and feeling tremendous guilt over what happened to the patient.

And it's likely that authorities will be able to trace the error back to her anyway—hospitals, after all, keep meticulous records about what was administered and by whom—and she could lose her job.

How much worse would it be for her if she stood up and admitted her error, got help for the patient right away, saved him from dying, and presented her action as an honest mistake for which she is personally accountable?

It wouldn't be worse.

She still might lose her job, but she'll know she stood up and did everything she could to right her own wrong. And the patient will be alive!

In our day-to-day lives, the consequences of our actions are hardly ever so drastic as they were for President Clinton, Mr. Libby, Ms. Stewart, or the nurse.

More likely, we miss a deadline because we cram too many commitments onto our calendars or we misjudge the potential of a young job candidate who turns out to wreak minor havoc around the office.

We can respond in one of two ways: First, and more common, is to weasel out of being responsible for the problem with the hope that we will escape the punishment that so often accompanies our being accountable: *I couldn't meet the deadline because the accounting department didn't get me the data I needed on time.* Or, *The new guy botched the job; he's incompetent!*

A better, more credible and accountable response might be: *I missed the deadline; I overbooked my calendar. I really thought I could get both projects finished on time, but I was wrong. I'm four days behind. I will not accept any new commitments until I finish what's already on my plate.* Or, *I can see that I misjudged the potential of the new guy. He's not working out as I expected. It's my role to let him go and to find a more suitable replacement.*

Now, was that so hard?

Yes!

It *is* hard. It's hard for us to admit that we were wrong or that we are personally accountable for something that turned out badly.

Here's why: We're rewarded for making excuses.

We live in a culture that punishes us for telling the truth and rewards us for hiding it.

If the nurse who dispensed the wrong medicine runs to the doctor to admit it, he probably will become angry with her, threaten to get her fired, and blame her if the patient dies.

If she keeps her secret, perhaps she can escape that kind of ire—and even keep her job.

In the long run, though, she pays a higher price by refusing to own up to her mistake: the death of a patient on her conscience for the rest of her life.

I'd rather get yelled at by an irate doctor than cause a patient to die. I'd rather get fired. I'd rather get sued.

Would you?

Maybe you believe it's better to lose your job than to kill a patient.

Maybe you don't.

Either way, own your belief. Be accountable for it.

It's yours. Stand up and be accountable for what's yours.

What If You Don't Get Caught?

Two Wednesdays in a row, after the lunch crowd thinned out and Nora, a waitress, was alone in the small, family-owned ice cream parlor where she had worked for two months, she stole $40 from the cash register.

Nobody saw her slip the two crisp twenty-dollar bills into her apron pocket either time. She used the money to buy her son a pair of sneakers he had begged for.

She didn't think anybody would miss the money. She was wrong.

The first week, nobody mentioned that the drawer came up short. The second week, it was short by the same amount, and the couple in charge called the shop's three waitresses together to ask them why.

Each one, at times, had been alone in the shop. Each one pleaded ignorance.

All three suffered when the couple, suspecting that one of them was a thief, put a halt to the free sodas and lunches the waitresses had always been allowed to enjoy.

The couple never treated any of the waitresses quite the same again. The friendly, family atmosphere instantly turned into one of suspicion and blame.

One of the other waitresses quit a few weeks later because she no longer enjoyed working there. Those who remained figured that proved she was the culprit, and things eventually got back to normal.

Nora felt badly about the other waitress and even worse that it was her dishonesty that started the trouble. Still, she never told what she did.

I won't ask you what you would have done. It would be too easy for you to take the high road and say you never would have stolen in the first place.

Instead, let me ask you this: Are you accountable for your actions if nobody holds you accountable?

Are you accountable for your actions if nobody catches you?

The people in your life, from your spouse to your kids to your boss to your clients, hold you accountable for the things you do that affect them.

Authorities in our society—the police, the courts, the IRS, teachers, lifeguards—hold you accountable for the things you do that affect the people around you.

What happens when nobody catches you?

Are you still accountable?

There is no Accountability Police. We police ourselves on our sometimes rocky, sometimes smooth journey toward personal success and happiness.

I'm going to answer my own question. What happens when nobody catches you? *You are still accountable.*

Yes, even if nobody catches you.

You are accountable for your behavior and choices, even if you refuse to stand up and say you are.

If you run a red light and the police pull you over, and you deny it, you're still accountable for your choice to run the red light.

Even if you don't get a ticket, you're still accountable.

If you slam on your brakes and cause the guy two cars back to ram into the back of the car in front of him, you can blame the guy behind you for tailgating. That doesn't mean you didn't cause the accident.

You're still accountable, even though he's the one who's going to wind up in traffic court.

If you're the kind of person who accepts the consequences of your own behavior—who behaves in an accountable way—you'll pull over and explain how your actions contributed to the wreck.

You won't speed away, feeling sly and happy in the knowledge that the last driver in the line is the one who will get the traffic ticket.

You'll be accountable for your actions and accept the consequences.

Yeah, right.

Why would you turn yourself in when you could get away scot-free?

Don't fool yourself. *You're still accountable.*

And you know it. Even if nobody else does.

Before I discovered how happy and successful I could be once I became personally accountable for all of my choices,

I might have pushed the blame for that fender-bender onto the guy behind me, too.

For some, maybe for you, their consciences would bid them to stay put, to 'fess up, to make sure nobody got hurt.

For me, my conscience doesn't have anything to do with it.

My sense of who I am, how I want to be and feel, and what's right for me are what dictate my willingness to risk getting a ticket of my own for driving recklessly.

I won't feel guilty if I flee the scene because I won't leave unless I know that is absolutely the right thing to do.

It's not an issue for me. It's not a hard choice because my choices are consistent. I choose accountability every single time.

If I pull over and confess that I slammed on my breaks and caused the accident, I won't later wish I hadn't taken responsibility. I know I have done the right thing for me.

That kind of mind-set and behavior obliterates feelings of guilt because there's nothing to feel guilty about.

I made a mistake, I admitted it, and I paid for it.

Period. I've moved on.

That mind-set saves so much time that I might have wasted arguing and accusing and blaming because there I am, announcing that I am accountable.

Who can argue with that?

I don't find fault, place blame, feel guilt, or try to make others feel guilty. That's what being accountable means.

I say, "Here's what I did, here's how it turned out, and here I am. Here's what is."

I'll apologize for causing the accident. I'll pay the fine. I'll take the points.

I'll feel badly for causing the accident.

Then we'll all go back to our lives.

Accountability means you take the glory when your choices have a happy ending, and you suffer the consequences, whatever they are, if they cause a problem.

Since I started living my life that way, I find that I suffer much less often than I used to.

I fail less often. I think, plan, and act—before I make a choice or empower myself to take an action—with the full knowledge that I will be fully accountable for the success or failure of the endeavor—after the fact.

I make an up-front decision to own it fully.

To that end, I take the actions that I believe are necessary to make everything I do a success. I work as hard as I can. I honor my commitment to the best of my capabilities. I do what I have to do in order to make sure I'm perfectly clear about what I need to do and what those who are counting on me expect of me. I do what I say I'm going to do.

Do you?

Own Your Choices—Right or Wrong

What if, for some reason, I hightailed it away from that accident scene before anybody could get my license plate number?

What if I believed that was the right thing for me?

I know I won't regret it later because I own that choice. *I'm still accountable.*

Maybe the guy in the other car pointed a gun at me and threatened to shoot me for causing the accident. So I sped away to save my life.

I can own that decision, even though it might look bad to those I leave behind.

My decisions might not be the same ones you would make. That's okay with me.

As long as you own yours.

As long as you own your choices and don't blame their outcomes on anyone else. As long as you answer for your own decisions and actions.

Say you rob a bank and you're speeding away and you slam on your brakes at a red light and cause an accident.

You know robbing banks is illegal and letting others take the fall when you cause an accident is mean. You choose to do it anyway.

You make your living robbing banks, and you make loads of money doing it. Getting away with robbery gives you the thrill you need to feel happy. You own your choice.

And there's no way you're going to get caught with the loot in your car because you couldn't outrun a traffic light. So you flee the scene.

You determine that's the right thing for you. You don't pretend it was someone else's fault. You own your choice.

Just because others don't like your choices doesn't mean you're not accountable for them.

Just because your choices have outcomes that displease others doesn't mean you aren't as accountable as I am.

Here's a more likely example.

After fifteen years of marriage, Tricia's husband left her and their three young sons when his year-long affair with another woman was discovered.

That was two years ago.

Tricia still hasn't filed for divorce, and in the state where she lives, only the wronged spouse may file for divorce. She doesn't have a financial settlement. She still wears her wedding ring. She hasn't looked for a job.

She lives every day as if Doug will be home for dinner at 6:00.

At first, her friends understood. Two years later, they don't.

They tell her to get a job, hire a bulldog divorce lawyer, and take the philandering scumbag to the proverbial cleaners. They suggest that dating would be a first step to starting a new life for herself and her sons.

They whisper to each other that they wish she would do *something* to move on with her life instead of complaining that Doug spends too much money or that his family doesn't invite her to their parties anymore.

They say she's not taking charge of her life, that she's acting like she's not responsible for what happens to her next.

They're wrong.

It's just as responsible to do nothing as it is to do something. Either way, you answer for it. You're accountable for your results.

Tricia's friends don't know what she should do. They know what *they* would do, or at least what they think they would do.

They don't approve of Tricia's choices or behavior, but she's accountable for the outcomes that result.

Surprised that the former Queen of Victims would endorse Tricia as she plays the victim card?

She knows what she's doing. Tricia *chooses* to play the victim. She wants Doug to be responsible for her. She doesn't want to support herself; she wants him to support her. She doesn't want a divorce; she wants to be Mrs. Doug—even if it makes her miserable because he clearly doesn't love her anymore.

She even knows that she's making herself miserable. It's her choice.

Support it or stay out of it.

Crystal Clear

Robert, a freelance writer, and Jody, the editor of an agricultural magazine, have worked together for four years, even though they've never met.

Jody feels comfortable assigning Robert to write about a broad topic and then letting him run with it. It saves her from spending her time nailing down a specific angle.

So when her publisher asks for a profile of a prominent midwestern secretary of agriculture, Jody assigns the story to Robert.

Robert knows the magazine usually goes easy on elected officials, but during an interview for the story, he asks the official to talk about his successes and failures, his plans and his challenges, and even about a scandal in his office.

Jody loves the story. But just as she's about to send the magazine to the printer, she gets a phone call from her angry publisher.

The agriculture secretary has called to complain that he didn't like Robert's questions.

He didn't want to talk about failures and challenges and the scandal.

He was expecting to talk only about his successes and the familiar story of his childhood on a dairy farm.

"You know we give state officials the soft treatment in the magazine," the irate publisher tells Jody. "What were you thinking?"

Jody hates publishing "fluff" stories about officials. She was thinking Robert would write a substantial story.

But she doesn't tell that to the publisher. She says, "I didn't write this story. A freelancer wrote it. He didn't ask the right questions."

She calls Robert to tell him he was supposed to write a "fluff" story and ask only soft questions.

Like Jody, Robert doesn't like "fluff."

ROBERT: Why do you want "fluff" this time when you haven't asked for that before?

JODY: We always go easy on public officials.

ROBERT: If that's what you wanted, you should have told me.

JODY: I thought you would have been able to figure that out because you're familiar with our magazine. I shouldn't have to tell you everything. You'll have to do the story over.

ROBERT: This isn't my fault. I did the assignment that you asked me to do. If you want me to do it over, you'll have to pay me more.

JODY: It *is* your fault. You should have asked me to clarify the assignment if you didn't understand it.

Jody is right; Robert should have asked for clarification.

Robert is right, too. Jody should have been clear from the beginning about what she wanted.

Who is accountable for this debacle?

Both of them. One hundred percent—each.

How could they have prevented the situation?

Robert could have asked Jody to be clear about what she expected from him for this assignment—and each new assignment.

Jody could have made it clear to Robert that he was to soft-pedal the story.

You already know that accountability has three prongs: personal responsibility (before the fact, you are 100 percent responsible for the success or failure of the task); self-empowerment (you empower yourself to take the risks you need to get the result you want); and personal accountability (after the fact, you stand up and admit that you're the genius behind what has just occurred—good or bad).

The lynchpin that binds the three prongs: clear agreements.

You can boil accountability down to one behavior: making things clear up front.

For you to be accountable, you need to be perfectly clear about what you expect from others and about what others expect from you.

If you are responsible for the success of a project, you must also empower yourself to be crystal clear about those two sets of expectations.

Making things clear involves making clear agreements.

If you are an accountable person, chances are you are consistent when it comes to five key behaviors. Accountable people:

1. Are absolutely clear about what they expect of others and about what others expect of them.
2. Make clear agreements.
3. Establish ownership for every task: They put a "who" with every "what," and always know "by when."
4. Keep to timelines and meet their deadlines; if that's not possible, they renegotiate before the due date.
5. Focus on results.

The next chapters discuss each of these important points in more detail.

Write It Down

Michelle teaches spinning classes at a local health club on Mondays, Wednesdays, and Saturdays.

She asks Tanya if she would be willing to take over the Saturday class every other week, starting in two weeks, when Michelle will be at her sister's wedding. Tanya agrees.

Tanya shows up the next week to teach the class. Michelle is already there.

"We agreed you would start *next* week," Michelle reminds Tanya.

"No, you asked me to come this week. I can't come next week."

"I can't come next week, either," Michelle says.

"Not my problem," Tanya retorts.

This is a simple example, but an all-too-common one with an equally common solution: Michelle could have shot Tanya a quick e-mail spelling out which dates each had agreed to teach the class.

Want to successfully negotiate a clear agreement? I have three words for you: *Write it down.*

You may be able to argue that you had an oral agreement, and that the other guy didn't honor it, but it will be hard to prove.

What good will it do if you can prove it, anyway? The misunderstanding, and the ensuing finger-pointing, have already occurred.

The deadline has already been missed.

Save yourself the trouble. Write it down.

Accountable people make clear agreements.

An effective agreement is written, and it clarifies who owns each part of a task. It includes what each person is expected to do and records a deadline for completing the work.

The agreement states, *Who will do what by when?*

Like a contract for building a house, the agreement is adopted by all parties involved, not just by an enforcer like a general contractor, who piles work on people without knowing whether they can fit the tasks into their schedules or whether they understand what's being asked of them.

Making clear agreements is the single most important behavior of the accountable person.

It's important to pin down your supervisor and all the members of your team so that each person knows his or her role and responsibility, how to accomplish it, and when it's due.

That way, every member of the team is responsible for holding every other member of the team accountable for what he or she has agreed to do.

The more personally accountable each person is, the less time the team spends "managing."

A clear agreement is a high-performance contract.

Follow these ten steps for every agreement you make with others, whether they are asking you to do something or you are asking them to do something:

1. Decide on the goal, task, or objective that your team will accomplish.
2. Brainstorm all of the activities "we" as a group need to do to accomplish the goal, task, or objective.
3. Each item on the list gets one owner, and each task gets a deadline. (It's not necessary for the "owner" of a task to accomplish it herself. She may delegate the task to someone else while being responsible for its completion and still will be personally accountable for its outcome.)
4. One member of the group agrees to be the "keeper of the contract" and records all of the agreements that are made, updating as needed. This is a clerical function, not a management role.
5. Not being at a meeting is not a reason to miss reporting on the status of your agreement. Have someone else do it for you.
6. If it looks like you won't be able to do the work by the deadline you agreed to, make arrangements with the group in advance. Explaining it *after* the deadline has passed is unacceptable and shows disregard for the group effort.
7. It's okay to renegotiate agreements during a progress report.

8. The success of high-performance contracting rests on self-management and keeping agreements.
9. If agreements are not being kept, it is up to the individual group members to figure out why. If that doesn't work, call in a manager to mediate. The more the group behaves this way, they less it needs a manager. This is how low-cost, high-quality organizations operate.
10. This process works for agreements between individuals as well as for agreements among team members. It even works as a tool for you to make an agreement with yourself.

Clear agreements involve written commitments—including *who will do what by when*—as well as buy-in from all participants in the project.

It's fine to begin a project with a simple conversation. But if you don't write the agreement down and get people to commit to specific tasks and to follow up with progress reports, the project is doomed.

And if leaders "opt out" of the contract because of their positions or titles, the project is doomed. It gives them the opportunity to make excuses like, "I'm too busy," or "I'm too important."

So don't *imply* your instructions; write them down.

Don't let others *imply* their commitments. Get them in writing, with a "by when" date for each.

Consider this statistic from an old management study: In 1994, 230,000 managers lost their jobs within six months of being promoted *because they did not understand their new roles.*

There was no clear agreement about what they were supposed to accomplish.

Here's how to get clear:

1. Describe the project you have taken ownership of.
2. Ask questions until you have a complete picture of what you're expected to accomplish, what result is expected, and what you're to deliver. Confirm your understanding. Write it down.
3. List everything you will do to complete the task and hand in your deliverables. Take the initiative to identify what kind of authority you'll need to do your job—and to get it. Ask for the assistance and resources that you'll need to do your best work.
4. Clarify the "by whens." If something is not assigned a date, it probably won't get done. Consider your deadline for the project as well as dates for important milestones and progress reports.
5. Put the project into perspective by learning why it's important. What's the reason for this project? The history behind it? Whom will it benefit if you complete the project well and on time? What's at stake if you don't? This information will help you and your team put your roles into context.
6. Fill out a Clear Agreement Form (you'll find one on the next page) and review it with everyone involved.

A clear agreement reaps far better results than an implied or casual agreement that leaves any part of the *who will do what by when* equation unassigned.

Clear agreements produce the desired results.

Write it down so everybody knows what the agreement is and buys into it.

THE CLEAR AGREEMENT FORM

Use *Exhibit 5* as a tool to help you take ownership for work to be done. Complete it on your own or with others who will work with you on a task.

There is no better way to confirm mutual understanding than to see something in black and white.

EXHIBIT 5. Clear Agreement Form

Owner: _____

1. What is the TASK?
   What is the task or project
   I am taking
   ownership of?

2. What is the OUTCOME
   or DELIVERABLE?
   Consider:
   Level of detail?
   Format?
   Measures or standards?
   Customer or end user of
   information, product, or service?

3. What ACTIONS will I take
   to complete the task?
   Consider:
   Others involved?
   Authority needed?
   Assistance needed?
   Resources needed?

(Continued)

EXHIBIT 5. (*Continued*)

4. What are the BY WHENs?
   What are the deadlines for
   this task?

5. What are the STAKES associated
   with this task?
   Benefits of completing?
   Consequences of not completing?
   Who will be affected?

A Clear Risk

Suppose Jody, the editor, had told Robert, the writer, when she made the assignment that he should take it easy on the agriculture secretary and write a story that ignored his failures and scandals.

What if Michelle had sent Tanya a written confirmation spelling out their agreement for the spinning classes?

Nobody would be in trouble and nobody would be pointing fingers.

What a difference a little clarity can make to the success or failure of a project!

Yet most people shy away from being perfectly clear about their expectations of others and about what others expect of them.

Do you? Think about *why*.

The reason is simple human nature: If I am perfectly clear about what I expect of you, and you don't come through, then I have to hold you accountable for messing everything up.

I don't want to do that.

I don't like confrontation, and that's what will happen if we have to discuss your failure to honor your commitment.

That's not going to be pleasant for either one of us; nobody likes that kind of conflict.

You can see how uncomfortable it got between Jody and Robert, who have always gotten along. Now they're arguing and blaming each other.

That's a typical reaction when something goes wrong. We set ourselves up for it.

If I am not clear about what I expect of you and you don't come through, we can both blame it on the lack of clear instructions (or you can blame it on me for not giving clear instructions, and I can blame it on you for not clarifying what you didn't understand).

That's better.

Not!

Sure, it gets us both off the hook. Sort of.

But it sure doesn't get the work done.

Jody was not clear with Robert about the assignment, and now she's got someone to blame. Robert didn't ask her for specific instructions, and now he's got someone to blame.

Great strategy.

It sure didn't get the work done.

Accountable people are absolutely clear about what they expect of others and about what others expect of them.

If you are accountable, you will get clear and be clear before the project begins.

But you won't have anyone to blame if the project fails.

Are you up for that?

Clarity is a huge risk.

You risk giving up your scapegoats. When everybody's clear, there's nobody to blame.

The next time you are responsible for something, take the risk to be absolutely clear.

You'll have no excuses available to you—and nobody to blame—if the project turns out badly or if you don't complete it as promised.

Everything was clear up front—you saw to that yourself.

Floating in We-We

The Literacy League's once-robust board of directors was down to four longtime members, who decided to recruit some younger volunteers for an infusion of fresh ideas.

It found those volunteers in Tracy and Mark, who arrived at their first meeting bursting with energy for the cause of teaching reading to illiterate adults.

They suggested holding an open house for potential volunteer reading tutors; asking a local sports hero to star in a public service announcement for TV; and contacting former tutors to reenlist them in the effort.

Everyone in the room embraced the ideas.

Tracy, a born organizer, whipped out her yellow legal pad and started writing.

"We've all agreed we'll hold an open house. What do we need to do to make that happen?"

"We could ask the church on 2nd Street if we can hold it in the meeting room," one director volunteered.

"We need to order refreshments," someone else said.

"Let's choose a date so we can all be there to mingle with the volunteers," another offered.

"Great," said Tracy. "Who will call the church?"

Nothing.

She looked at the director who suggested the church. "Will you call the church?" she asked.

"No, I don't have time to do anything like that," he replied.

"Who then?"

Nothing.

"Who will order the sodas and cookies?" she asked, and looked at the person who had the idea.

"I can't do that; I have to work all day," the director said.

This went on for about 10 minutes, until Tracy said, "We all agreed we would do this. Who did you think would do the work?"

Everybody stared at their shoes.

In fact, the directors didn't care who did the work as long as it wasn't them.

Sound familiar?

When "we" agree to do something, it doesn't get done.

A "we" unowned is a job undone.

Accountable people establish ownership for every task. They put a "who" with every "what."

It is critical to identify the "who" part of *who will do what by when.*

Everyone has been to meetings at which a table of bright, enthusiastic team members or volunteers offers one great idea after the other—any or all of which might solve a problem, raise money, right a wrong, or change the organization's culture for the better.

"We" can do this; it will be great!

"We" could make a videotape of managers who supervise telecommuters so other supervisors could hear the benefits.

"We" could put a comment box outside of each manager's office and advertise it to employees. What a great way to get input and ideas from the rank-and-file!

"We" could send an invitation to our annual meeting to anyone who has retired from the company for the past five years. That will give us a chance to see if any of them want to return to work part-time to help us during this recruiting crunch.

Those are all great ideas.

Now the team leader has a big question to ask: *Who* will make the videotape? *Who* will post the suggestion box? *Who* will send the invitation?

The inevitable response: Not *me!*

The problem with most meetings is that they're full of we-we.

We need to do this, *we* need to do that. *We* need some more data. *We* need to form a committee.

By the end of a meeting like that, I feel like I need a raft to float on because I'm floating out of this meeting in all the we-we.

Here's my solution: Change the we-we to do-do.

I will do this task. *I* will be responsible.

I will arrange for the videotape by a week from Friday. *I* will buy a suggestion box this afternoon and ask the building crew to hang it near the first-floor elevator by the end of the week. *I* will compile a list of retirees' names and make invitations for them by the 23rd, in plenty of time for them to go out before the annual meeting.

I will take action. *I* will do it. *I* will answer for it.

You don't have to do every task yourself. Secure commitments from everyone in the room.

If you don't, maybe "we" will get it done.

Someday, maybe.

Or never.

"We" *never* gets it done.

Someone at the meeting can do it, but "we" can't do it. "We" isn't specific.

"We" implies that "one of us" will do it, but it doesn't specify which one.

That means I'm going to leave it to you, and you're going to leave it to me.

"We" are going to leave it undone.

"We" are going to let our ideas remain as only ideas, not actions, unless each of us is responsible for saying, "I will do this part of the task by a certain date. I own it. You can count on me. I will be personally accountable."

Then *you* get it done. *I* get it done.

In an effective meeting, a specific person assigns or accepts ownership for each part of a task.

Embroider this on a pillow and put it in a place where you'll see it every day:

A "we" unowned is a job undone.

Who is *we?*

For starters, *you.*

Identify yourself. Say what you're able to take on and when you can be finished.

Then put the rest of the team on the spot: "*Who* will do this task? By when? What can the rest of us do to support you in owning that?"

It could be that nobody will step up and accept ownership for parts of the task. That doesn't mean your role is to shoulder it all yourself.

Say so.

I will not do the entire project alone. I will do this part by this date. Who will do the rest?

Empower yourself. Take the risk. Press the point.

Solicit ownership, but don't "volunteer" or assign your teammates to jobs they do not want.

To say someone "should" do something is about as effective as promising that "we" will get it done.

The Literacy League directors do that all the time: We *should* do this! Tracy, you *should* do it.

When you "should" on someone, prepare yourself to land in a big pile of "should."

"Should" stinks up the place. You need tall rubber boots to step over it.

- "You *should* stop doing that."
- "You *should* be more clear."
- "You *should* do more to contribute to this project."

Telling someone what she "should" do is no guarantee that she will do it.

You know this: When someone tells you what you should do, do you run out and do it? No!

You do what you *agree* to do, not what someone else *thinks* you should do.

You might even agree that you should do it. That doesn't mean you will.

Each person needs to decide she is responsible for the success of the project and then get clear on her role.

A manager or your teammates or your spouse can tell you that you are responsible for a task, but only you can determine the truth of this. It's *your* mind-set, not theirs.

Only you can empower yourself to take the risks and actions necessary to get the job done.

Only you can stand up after all is said and done and say, "The buck stops here. I'm accountable."

Whether you *should* do those things is irrelevant.

Same goes for the people you're "should-ing" on. You can't *make* someone else responsible.

So stop "should-ing" on people! It's not going to accomplish anything.

Here's proof. One of my clients, a health care management analyst at a university hospital, wrote this:

I am so tired of *should*.

We never know where we are because we are so busy trying to should our way to somewhere in the Land of Some Day, on the Planet of Nowhere.

And most of the time we can't even find our way back to square one because we have should it away!

Just in Time

The leader of a hospital's Information Technology (IT) Team holds a meeting to get started on a project that will let physicians enter orders for medications into a computer instead of scratching them in illegible handwriting onto a prescription pad.

The team leader explains to the six team members that the new system could reduce the number of medication errors and even save lives.

The enthusiastic team brainstorms all afternoon and identifies five main tasks that it must accomplish in order to put the system in place:

1. Find out what software exists. Can the hospital buy something that fits its needs, or will the IT staff have to write its own program?

2. Tweak the program so the computer will cross-check every medicine ordered for a patient with every other medicine that patient is already taking.
3. Add to the program so it will raise a red flag if a doctor orders an unusually high dose of a medicine or a medicine that is not usually prescribed for the patient's symptoms.
4. Install the new program on computers at every nurse's station in the hospital.
5. Teach the staff how to use the new program.

So far, so good.

Pleased with the list, the team leader asks each of the five other members to choose an area for which he or she will be responsible.

After some negotiating, each member accepts ownership of one of the areas, and the meeting adjourns.

In a week, the team leader calls another meeting to ask team members for progress reports.

One member has counted the number of nursing stations that will need computers, but has not collected prices on new computers. Another has contacted a national hospital bench-marking organization to get information about usual doses of medicine.

Nobody else has any progress to report.

Stop here for a moment. Does this surprise you?

Read on.

The team leader becomes angry, saying everyone agreed to do the work. He demands to know why they haven't done it.

The team members are stunned by his anger. They tell him the truth.

"We didn't know you wanted us to do the work by today."

"We thought we had more time."

"We were going to do it later."

"We were busy this week."

"We didn't write this on our calendars."

In fact, they may or may not have done the work later. Something else—something with a definite deadline—always would have found a place on their calendars ahead of this team project.

The work that's due is the work that gets done.

The team leader had not assigned deadlines for specific tasks or declared a time frame in which to complete the project.

Now, the team has to involve a manager, and everything is a rush job.

Accountable people keep to timelines and meet their deadlines.

They don't need to be managed.

Hand in hand with the "who" comes the "when" in a clear agreement.

Who will do what by when?

Agreeing to a deadline—whether you're the one doing the work or the one assigning it—is critical to the success of any project.

Suppose the leader of the hospital IT team had assigned the team members to do their initial research and come back with a solid recommendation by a week from Friday.

Chances are, all of them would have had something to report.

Just as important as it is to establish a timeline for each task, it is equally critical for each member of the team to honor those time commitments. An accountable team will declare up front what the consequence is for missing a deadline.

The accountable team knows that if one of its members fails, the whole team fails.

Especially when an individual is part of a team effort, a missed deadline by one can delay the work of another.

If I can't book the training room until we know which day the computers will arrive, your failure to order the computers on time interrupts the flow of the project.

If I don't know which kind of computers to order until you decide on the software package, and you put your decision off, that interrupts the flow of the project.

Disregarding deadlines disrespects the other members of the team and shows a lack of personal responsibility for the success of the project.

Most of us don't simply blow off our deadlines; they just have a way of sneaking up on us quicker than we realized.

Perhaps the task turns out to take twice as long as you expected.

Maybe you sincerely believed you could handle everything on your calendar, but it turns out you had too much work.

You can learn from the experience of a missed deadline, but that doesn't do your team much good right now.

What *does* help is realizing you've made a scheduling error, approaching your team, and renegotiating your deadline—well before deadline day.

That way, those who are counting on you know what to expect and can plan their own calendars accordingly.

Rolling Heads

Heads are going to roll!"

Jim says that so often at work that his staff mimics him behind his back.

They imagine their chopped-off heads rolling all over the office floor. They joke that Jim would have to cuff his pants legs up to his knees and hop over them as if he were crossing a creek on stepping stones that wobbled underfoot.

Jim looks for someone to blame every time something goes wrong.

After his boss took him to task for comments he made to a company director, he chastised Leslie for saying the same thing to him in a casual conversation.

After he lost his cool during a client meeting and lost the account, he blamed his wife for letting him oversleep so he missed breakfast and felt poorly during the meeting.

Jim's excuses don't absolve him of his actions, of course, and they don't change the fact that the choices that led to those actions were Jim's, and not Leslie's or Mrs. Jim's.

Jim is not accountable.

Accountable people spend their time taking the actions necessary to reach their goals and get their work done. They don't spend time placing blame or finding fault.

They practice the 85% Solution. They know that they alone are responsible for their successes and failures.

As a member of a team whose project is not going as planned, an accountable person does not point fingers or try to find out who caused the meltdown.

Instead, the accountable team member asks, "What is the problem, and how can each team member contribute to solving it, starting with me?"

Accountable people focus on results.

In fact, accountable people—those who are 100 percent responsible for the success of the endeavor—look first to themselves to see if they are contributing to the problem or can offer a solution.

They ask themselves these four questions:

1. What is the problem?
2. What am I doing or not doing that is contributing to the problem?
3. What will I do differently in an effort to solve the problem?
4. How will I be accountable for the result?

They ask those questions instead of asking, "Whose fault is this? Why did you do that? Are you out of your mind?"

They ask those questions instead of yelling, "Heads are going to roll!"

It takes a lot of time to figure whose fault something is or why someone made a bad choice.

The answers to the second set of questions are not going to get the task finished or corrected.

Finding those answers will waste time, cause hard feelings, and further disrupt the work.

Forget whose fault it is.

Who will do what by when this time around?

Solve the problem, don't compound it.

Let your teammates be right, even if it means they say you are wrong.

Respond, "Okay, I'll be wrong. Now, let's get back to work."

Sticks and Stones

Count the number of people you know who live by those five principles of personal accountability:

1. Be absolutely clear about what you expect of others and about what others expect of you
2. Make clear agreements
3. Establish ownership for every task: Put a "who" with every "what," and always know "by when."
4. Keep to timelines and meet their deadlines; if that's not possible, renegotiate before the due date.
5. Focus on results.

Chances are you've got plenty of fingers and toes left over.

Accountability is crucial to the success of any project, organization, or relationship, yet few people hold themselves or others accountable, even if they believe that doing so will make efficient work out of even a complicated chore.

Here's why: When a manager holds an employee accountable—even if the manager has been fair and the employee obviously has shirked his responsibility—how is that manager perceived?

"He's mean."

"She's holding me accountable."

"It's about time some of these people were held accountable."

"Oh, no! She's been to one of Linda Galindo's seminars!"

If you hold others accountable—and ask them to hold you accountable—you could find yourself ridiculed.

The people you're holding accountable might resist you.

That means you're doing it right!

Women, in particular, have a hard time with this.

Even women who easily grasp the concepts of responsibility and accountability sometimes find it hard to act on them.

A woman doesn't want to be thought of or called a wicked witch (or something that rhymes).

I've been called worse. So what?

If your staff or colleagues or anyone else calls you a witch, it's probably because they're not used to holding themselves accountable or being held accountable for their actions and inactions.

What? Ask someone to honor a commitment or a written agreement? To sit down and get clear up front about who will do what by when?

You *witch!*

Perhaps they think your job is to make grown men cry . . .

A friend of mine who teaches college in the East told me about an anonymous course evaluation from a student who wrote, "If you were a bird, you would eat your own young."

She knew immediately who had written it: the student who, all semester, told her she was "going to make me lose my scholarship" and accused her of "flunking me."

He never acknowledged his role in the unfortunate D he received in the course—that he skipped several classes, neglected to turn in a major assignment, and never bought the textbook, saying, without reading it, that it was "a waste of money."

Still, the teacher held him accountable, telling him repeatedly, "You're going to have to repeat this course if you do not do X, Y, and Z," and then assigning him a D—a grade too low to apply to his chosen degree—when he didn't comply.

The young man refuses to hold himself accountable. He's too busy telling his friends and his parents, "It's not my fault. I blame my teacher. I had nothing to do with it. I'm not accountable."

On the other hand, the teacher *is* accountable.

She could do what's popular—hand out undeserved As and Bs—instead of demanding the hard work that she believes is better for college students than a free ride—and never endure the name calling.

She empowers herself to assign poor grades to students who do poor work. She chooses to take the risk that she will be hated or ridiculed.

She knows the dean reads the student evaluations, too, without having any insight into the student's semester-long behavior. It's another risk she chooses to take because she is responsible for the education of her students.

She'll accept the consequence of being branded as strict or even as a bird who would eat her own young.

Or as a wicked witch.

So what? Only sticks and stones will break her bones.

In the end, she—and you, if you choose to hold yourself accountable for your actions—will be perceived by most (and probably eventually, even by the angry student) as effective, fair, consistent, clear, supportive, a good listener, and someone who is willing to explain her rationale and answer questions.

That's not a bad way to be perceived.

But in the beginning—when you begin to switch your habit from not holding people accountable to holding them accountable—the perception of those around you might not be so positive.

You might be perceived in a negative way because you're choosing to do this.

That has to be okay with you, though, in order to stick it out long enough to see the positive results.

Is it okay with you?

Can you say, "So what?" when someone calls you a witch (or worse)?

In the practice of personal accountability, there will be a few negative comments lobbed at you to your face or about you behind your back.

Sometimes, being effective means you will not be liked in the way you're used to being liked.

Still, you'll be respected. And you'll respect yourself.

And you'll be okay—with yourself.

Holding Others Accountable

T here are boundaries for holding *others* accountable.

There are things you might do when you're holding people accountable that simply will not work.

Among them: intimidation, a demanding or condescending tone, a lack of understanding or an unwillingness to listen.

Ever notice that when you yell at people, or threaten, blame, or accuse them, they push back instead of responding to your concern?

APPROACH: "You shouldn't have talked to her like that!"

RESPONSE: "Well, you shouldn't talk to me like this!"

APPROACH: "If you don't do what I say, I'll cut you out of my will!"

RESPONSE: "Go right ahead."

If those approaches aren't working for you, find out what does.

Here's a place to start: Create an environment where it's okay for people to ask you questions and where it's okay for your employees/spouse/children/coworkers to hold you accountable as well.

It's never easy to tell someone she's not doing a good job.

It's uncomfortable to ask someone why he didn't do what he said he was going to do.

Before you do either, know what you're going to say. Prepare for the conversation—whether it's with a loved one or an employee—just as carefully as you would prepare for an important meeting with a client.

Here are three effective steps to take as you prepare to hold someone accountable:

1. Review the agreement you made with the person. Did you make your expectations clear? Did the other person agree to do the work, or did you tell her she *should* or *had* to? Did you overlook unmet agreements in the past, which might have led the person to expect you would overlook it this time, too? In what way did *you* contribute to the poor results you have to address?
2. Identify the problem. Is it an unmet deadline? Low productivity? Sloppy work? Where is the gap in performance that you want to discuss during a conversation about accountability? Prepare to give specific examples.
3. Schedule a time for your conversation. Don't do it when you're in a hurry or the other person is running off to a meeting. Find a quiet, private place where nobody will overhear or interrupt your discussion.

Now it's time for you to hold the person accountable. Here are four guidelines for your conversation:

1. State the purpose of the conversation, right up front. Let the other person know that you are not there to place blame or find fault. This approach will set the tone for a constructive meeting rather than a combative one.
   - Focus on mutual benefits. *Let's figure out what happened so the project will be a success. That's what's important to both of us.*
   - Say you want to solve the problem.
   - Treat the other person with respect.
2. Compare what you both agreed to with what actually happened. Do this without using the word *should*. Shoulds are all about blame. Instead, focus on facts and What *Is*, not What *Should Be*. What are the differences between the agreement and the actual results?
   - Explain how the person's actions affected you and others. Did it contribute to your missing a deadline, too? Did it cause you stress and worry? *I had hoped to have this wrapped up before the holidays so the staff wouldn't have it hanging over their heads during the busiest time of the year.*
   - Own up to your own role in the problem. *I didn't ask for progress reports between the time I made the assignment and the time the work was due. I can see now that progress reports might have helped keep the work on schedule.*
   - Have a "you-ectomy." Replace "you," which sounds like blame and accusations, with "I" in your conversation: *I'm surprised this project wasn't completed on time, given*

that we scheduled a full month between assignment and deadline.

3. Listen to the other person's response—without interrupting. It's tempting to cut off an explanation when the person says something you don't agree with. But if you listen patiently, you'll probably learn what went wrong—which is valuable information that will help you craft a new, more successful agreement with the person.

   A tip: People who refuse to hold themselves accountable very often pretend to be confused about or even unaware of the things you are holding them accountable for. Don't fall for it—but hold your tongue until the other person has had her say.
   - Don't jump to conclusions.
   - Ask questions if you need the other person to clarify something he has said.
   - If the other person becomes emotional, acknowledge that: *I can see this is upsetting . . . Take your time.*
   - Don't let the conversation stray from the problem at hand. Focus on current and future performance.

4. Make a new agreement—one that is perfectly clear— and move forward. There are those words again: *clear agreement*. High performance and accountability revolve around clear agreements.

   The agreement you started with clearly didn't work, so make a better one this time. Identify what went wrong and what you and the other person can do differently now in order to finish the job.
   - Ask the person to suggest ways to rectify the situation.
   - Clearly state the consequences—including the impact on you and others—if the new agreement isn't met.

- Talk about how to avoid the same problems this time around and in the future.
- Invite the other person to summarize what you have talked about and what the new agreement is.
- *Write it down.*

You will reap huge rewards—in the form of better performance from those you hold accountable—if you do this even 10 percent better than you did before you picked up this book.

Below, you'll find a worksheet you can use to prepare for holding others accountable.

HOLDING OTHERS ACCOUNTABLE

Use *Exhibit 6,* the Preparation Worksheet, to capture your thoughts in preparation for a conversation to hold someone accountable. Be specific. Script out key words and phrases.

EXHIBIT 6. Preparation Worksheet

How will you express the purpose of the conversation?

_____

_____

_____

_____

_____

(Continued)

EXHIBIT 6. (*Continued*)

What will you say to compare the original clear agreement
with actual results?

_____

_____

_____

_____

_____

What will you say and do to demonstrate patient listening?

_____

_____

_____

_____

What questions will you ask to understand the other person's
perspective?

_____

_____

_____

_____

EXHIBIT 6. (*Continued*)

What ideas do you have to produce better results in the future?

_____

_____

_____

_____

_____

To Thine Own Self
Be Clear

Do you keep the promises you make to yourself?

Even when nobody else is around?

Do you sneak a dessert and figure you'll get back on your diet tomorrow, and then blame your slow metabolism for keeping you overweight?

Have you cheated on your spouse because you found yourself in a place where nobody knows you and where nobody you know could ever find out, and then blame it on the three martinis you drank to get up the nerve to do it?

Did you get something for free because a store clerk forgot to charge you for it and figure it's the clerk's fault for being careless?

Do any of those excuses make you less overweight, less of an adulterer, or not a thief—because nobody caught you?

If your answer is *yes,* and that's okay with you, it's okay with me.

But if you don't want to be any of those things, start honoring the commitments you have made to yourself.

Do you consider yourself an honest, honorable person? Why?

Is it because you don't cheat on your wife? Is it because you don't make excuses when you gain weight?

Is it because you hold yourself accountable and admit—at least to yourself—that when you do something dishonest or dishonorable it's because you *chose* to do it?

Keep yourself on the path you want to live on by getting clear about what that path is.

Decide what you hope to accomplish (today, in life, in each situation) and why.

Know what you have to do to accomplish it.

And make a clear agreement with yourself.

Agree to hold yourself accountable, even when nobody else is around to see you screw up.

If you're serious about being accountable in your workplace, at home, at your community meetings, or anywhere, start with yourself.

If you're going to hold others accountable, hold yourself accountable first.

Allow others to hold you accountable.

Work is a good place to start.

Go to your supervisor with three things you want to work on, and ask for his or her support. A place to start:

- *I am not going to gossip anymore.* Please hold me accountable if I do.

- *I am not going to hold a "meeting after the meeting"*—the informal gathering of just a few who linger after the official meeting has ended to discuss, override decisions, and criticize what went on. Please hold me accountable as soon as you see me doing this.
- *I am going to listen* when people come to me with questions or concerns. Please hold me accountable if I fail to do that.

Announcing your intentions to others—friends, a spouse, coworkers, or a supervisor—will help you on your journey to self-accountability.

It's like sharing your definition of success with others: You'll be more likely to stick with it if others know you're trying to.

It's like dieting: If you do it secretly, it's too easy to cheat. If you tell others of your plan, they'll be in your face as soon as you order dessert.

There will be times when you wished you had kept your big mouth shut so you *could* indulge, but in the end, those who share your secret will become a support group for you, helping you honor your own intentions and find your way to personal accountability that will lead you to success.

Once you start on that road, others will follow. It's almost as if they don't have a choice.

Like the pebble that ripples across a pond, what you do will cause someone else to change in the same way.

If you stand up and say, "I'm going to be accountable, even if nobody else is," someone else will be accountable, too.

If you don't stand up, you're just as good as running in place.

If you rationalize your inaction by saying, "I can't do this because nobody else is doing it," you'll never move forward.

So what if nobody else is doing it? If you wait for everybody else to change, you'll be waiting a long, long time.

It's within your control to be 100 percent responsible for your own success every minute of every day.

It's within your control to empower yourself to do what you have to do to make that success happen.

It's within your control to be accountable for your own success.

Take control. *Be* in control.

Or don't, and be a victim.

Which are you?

Want to be sure? Make a clear agreement with yourself every time you make a commitment to do something.

Write it down.

Ask yourself these four questions:

1. What, exactly, am I agreeing to take ownership of?
2. What actions will I take to accomplish this objective? Will I work with others toward a common goal? How will I get the authority I need to get the job done? If I need help, how will I get it and from whom? How will I get the resources I need to complete the task?
3. By when will I finish this? What deadline did I agree to?
4. What are the consequences if I don't pull this off—well and on time? How will it affect me, my reputation, or my success? How will it affect others or my organization?

Just as it's important to be 100 percent clear with the people you will hold accountable, being perfectly clear with yourself—and writing it down so you won't have any excuses later—is a tactic of an accountable person.

Making clear agreements with yourself means you can hold yourself accountable, even if nobody else does.

The Accountability Quotient, Part 3

Being accountable for your actions means showing that you are willing to answer for the outcomes that result from your choices, behaviors, and actions.

This chapter will help you measure your "after-the-fact" ownership for results produced, the extent to which you will answer for your results, good or bad, contribute to a "blameless culture," and seek solutions.

On *Exhibit 7*, use a scale from zero to 5 (zero is "none" and 5 is "100 percent") to rate your own sense of how accountable you are for the results of your choices, behaviors, and actions. (The guidelines following the table will help you interpret your result.)

EXHIBIT 7. Your Personal Accountability Quotient

Category	Best Possible	Accumulated Score
Personal Accountability		*50*
Questions	*Rating Distribution*	

1. I am accountable for the results I produce, even if there is not enough time.

   0   1   2   3   4   5

2. I don't make excuses or blame others when something goes wrong at work.

   0   1   2   3   4   5

3. I am accountable for the results I produce, even if I am not provided with the resources I need.

   0   1   2   3   4   5

4. I am persistent about getting feedback about my interpersonal skills.

   0   1   2   3   4   5

5. I seek training opportunities for personal and professional growth on a regular basis.

   0   1   2   3   4   5

6. I have high self-esteem.

   0   1   2   3   4   5

7. I am accountable for the results I produce even if a situation is unfair.

   0   1   2   3   4   5

8. I encourage others to live up to their full potential in spite of the difficulties they may experience.

   0   1   2   3   4   5

EXHIBIT 7. *(Continued)*

Category	Best Possible	Accumulated Score
Personal Accountability		50
Questions	*Rating Distribution*	

9. When I hold coworkers accountable they do not feel personally attacked.	0	1	2	3	4	5
10. The work environment has the least to do with determining my level of productivity.	0	1	2	3	4	5

INTERPRET YOUR SCORE

High

If your responses add up to between 40 and 50, you are the embodiment of the 85% Solution! Your score (85% to 100%) reveals that you are an accountable person. Employers are looking for you.

Medium

Your score of between 30 and 40 reveals that you are receptive to cleaning up your act in the area of being accountable and holding others accountable. Do it. You are 70% to 84% there already.

Low

A score of between 0 and 30 indicates that you are not an accountable person. If you are getting the rewards you want for being a victim, finger-pointing and blaming, keep it up. But if you are tired of the road you are on, enlist the support of a coach and get busy with defining success for yourself as a first step. Your score of 0% to 69% is considered low.

Epilogue

The problems that exist in the world today cannot be solved
by the level of thinking that created them.

—*Albert Einstein*

An elderly woman spills hot coffee on herself after balancing her paper coffee cup between her knees in a car and then blames the restaurant that sold it to her for her burns. A successful lawyer sues a group of Atlantic City casinos for $20 million after she lost her home and her practice because of her gambling addiction.

The coffee case famously put a few hundred thousand dollars into the 79-year-old's pockets; the gambler's claim was thrown out of court.

Yet both point to a growing problem in our society: We don't want to hold ourselves accountable for our actions.

Corporate board members say it's not their fault if the accountants they hired covered up a financial scandal, even as they line their own pockets while their employees watch their life savings disappear. Investors say they are victims when they lose their fortunes to a scam artist who reported unfathomable high returns, even as they knew those reports couldn't be on the level. Homeowners who borrow more than they could ever imagine repaying blame the banks who lent them the money. And bankers who lent more money than their customers could possibly afford, in turn, blame their downward spiral in part on the homeowners who defaulted on those loans.

Some of these finger-pointers suffered great losses, but some reaped rewards for *not* being accountable—money or a lighter punishment or a bailout or even getting off scot-free.

Somewhere along the way, our society crossed a line and began rewarding us for not being accountable. Somewhere along the way, our culture started punishing us for making honest mistakes and then standing up and owning those mistakes.

To avoid that punishment, we resorted to blaming others for choices that we made ourselves.

It's got to stop.

You can stop it.

Decide that you will not get sucked into the vortex of finger-pointing and blame that pervades our culture. Decide that you will be accountable for your own choices and behavior, and that you will hold those near to you accountable for theirs.

Decide that you will support others who demonstrate personal accountability. Decide that you will look to them as role models as they encourage you to dig deep and reconnect with your moral compass.

A lack of personal accountability is a choice.

Accountability is yours to own. If you abandon it, own your choice.

On the other hand, if you choose accountability and I choose accountability, and then one by one more and more of us stand up and say, "I'm accountable," we can live in a society that *rewards* accountability. We can thrive with a government whose officials are accountable for their decisions; with a legal system that doesn't punish *you* for *my* mess; with a country-wide culture that expects honesty and forgives honest mistakes.

If we don't, the future is predictable. Just look behind you.

You can keep doing what hasn't worked for you in the past if you want to, but it's not going to work for you in the future, either.

Frankly, I don't understand anyone's choice to abandon accountability, even if it means getting away with something.

It's going to catch up with you. I guarantee it.

A lack of personal accountability is at the heart of chronic stress. It saps us of productivity. It wastes our time. It makes us less satisfied with our jobs, our relationships, and ourselves.

If you have taken the lessons of *The 85% Solution* to heart, you're probably nodding knowingly because you agree that personal accountability is sorely lacking and badly needed in our lives and in our society.

What you can do—today—is be accountable *yourself*. Be the answer to your own problems. Be the fulfillment of your own dreams.

Live the 85% Solution. It works.

The Author

Since 1995, Linda Galindo has been influencing organizations in diverse industries throughout the United States providing keynotes, consulting, seminars, and practical strategies to create accountable work cultures, interdisciplinary teams, and work environments of mutual respect. She receives top ratings at conferences nationwide, with enthusiastic referrals that make her a highly sought-after keynote provider, consultant, and culture change facilitator.

Linda does more than speak and inspire. With humor, expansive analysis, examples from her personal journey as an executive, and a keen understanding of the riveting issues facing the health care industry, she brings about important changes that lead to sustained, measurable improvement. Linda's remarkable insight comes at a time when organizations are under enormous pressure to deliver more for less and when the "new rules" in the global economy demand better teamwork not only to survive but to thrive.

Linda's work is fresh, original, and innovative. When a well-respected organizational development consultant writes, "In my fifteen years of training and development I've never had a speaker deliver such an impact that caused an instant behavior change in myself," it becomes obvious that Linda's messages are not only effective but trigger real and lasting change.

Accountability is a particularly pertinent topic in organizations today. Linda ensures this fundamental concept is weaved into every presentation in an immediately useful way. CRM Learning published Linda's work in a best-selling educational film *Accountability That Works!* now available worldwide. Linda also made her acclaimed seminar on *High-Performance Accountability* available as an audio CD for use as a refresher tool. Her book *Way to Grow!* is available on Amazon.com.

Linda has received many awards for her speaking and business acumen. In 2002, the National Association of Women Business Owners–Utah chapter named her the Woman Business Owner of the Year. She has served on the executive board of the United Way, Salt Lake City, as the chair of board development. Additionally, she is a faculty member for the Governance Institute and the Medical Leadership Institute. Linda serves on the board of NASBA's Center for the Public Trust.

Index

VERSERA™
PERFORMANCE CONSULTING

Experience the Power of Accountability
Versera Performance Consulting offers a top-down consultative approach to building accountability within organizations through a powerful assessment process, one-on-one coaching and facilitated accountability workshops.

Accountability In Action: Clear and Measurable Results
When organizations practice true accountability they develop cultures of empowered employees who are individually and collectively committed to organizational results.

You can expect to see:
- **Increased Productivity**: People can do more when agreements are clearly negotiated, monitored and fulfilled.
- **Enhanced Customer Satisfaction**: Customers appreciate knowing they can count on service providers to do what they say they will do.
- **Reduced Expenses**: Rework, redundancy and "babysitting" are reduced when employees at all levels of the organization understand the concepts of responsibility, self-empowerment and accountability.
- **Greater Job Satisfaction**: Improved working relationships and smoother functioning processes make each individual's work dramatically more rewarding.
- **Improved Marketing Perception**: Your brand and image are enhanced when everyone in the organization adopts the mindset and skills associated with 100% accountability.

Contact Versera at: www.verseraconsulting.com or (877) 958-8300

JB JOSSEY-BASS™
An Imprint of ⊕WILEY
Now you know.